F. Barton Davis

PASSING IT ON

A ROAD MAP FOR THE FIRST
52 WEEKS OF YOUR NEW LIFE

Magi
media
publications

www.magimedihub.com

D1211952

Passing It On

Copyright © 2009 by F. Barton Davis
Published by Magi Media Publications
P. O. Box 332
Pelham Al 35124

Printed in the United States
Cover design: CGKmdia
Interior design: CGKmedia

ISBN 978-0-9819502-2-8

To Granddad, Dad, Uncle Jr., Uncle Frank, Uncle Clint, Randy Davis, Scott Davis, John Brush, Craig Cornish, Frazier Green, Sam Powell, Don Burroughs, Steve Sapp and every other man who has served as a mentor to me over the years. Thank you for loving me and for letting God use you.

Contents

FOREWARD

There is something very special about family culture, history, genealogy, and family tradition. With a background in music, I've had the opportunity to be invited to weddings and events of various ethnicities. I've attended traditional African weddings, Jewish, and Russian ceremonies, to name a few. I've always been amazed, not growing up in a traditional family myself, at the passing on of family culture. There is a healthy sense of pride, confidence, and strength that comes from knowing where you're from, who you are, and where you're going. Your family's values and ideals have helped to shape past and present generations, and once ingrained in you, they will help to shape future ones as well. There is power in passing it on **(Mt 28:20).**

The Church is a family. It has a unique role to deposit the culture of Christ in every member. Its biggest task is not just reaching new converts but passing on a rich gospel record and intrinsic understanding of God. When these are deeply embedded in our hearts, it compels us to proclaim Him boldly.
In his book, Passing It On, Frank Davis has done a wonderful job of showing how to plant the values, culture, and ideals of Christ into the hearts of young Christians. These fifty-two studies assist in jump-starting the new convert on to maturity, extending deep roots, and building a culture of Christ.

As Frank's brother, I've known him all of my life. It is a remarkable thing to have a brother-brother in God's Kingdom. It is a great blessing. I am so very proud of him and how God has used his life. Like his life, you'll find the studies in this book challenging, provocative, and inspiring. For new Christians, these are valuable lessons for understanding their new life and family. For mature Christians, these are invaluable reminders of our deep family roots. Whichever the case, this book will leave you inspired to Pass It On!

Scott Davis
Evangelist
Queens New York

Introduction

For years, there has been speculation on whether a human child has ever been raised by wolves. Myths are full of stories that make this claim. One of the most famous of these is the ancient Roman tale of Romulus and Remus, but there are many others. There are even numerous accounts of people who have found feral children that they believe were raised by packs in the wild (a fairly recent case was reported from Russia in 2007). Most experts agree, that while highly unlikely, a wolf-child is possible. Still, even though there has been much speculation, no one has been able to prove an actual case, so until someone does, we're still waiting for the first human child to be successfully raised to maturity by wolves. Personally, I can't wait to see the Larry King interview.

Why will that be a big deal, a historic occasion? Simple. Wolves don't raise people. They eat people. Leaving your infant child at the doorstep of your local wolf is a bad adoption plan. Is it possible that they'll survive? Maybe. But the most likely scenario is that tragedy will come from abandoning a child to the wild. Only the cruelest human being would ever do such a thing, and no society could survive if such heartless action were its unofficial parenting strategy.

With that being the case, why are so many new converts left to fend on their own, cast aside while a prowling lion, Satan (I Peter 5:8), sizes them up. It is so exciting when someone is born again, becoming a new creation. In most cases, we went to great lengths to convert him or her, Bible studies, late night prayer, campaigns, revivals, mission teams, etc., but many, too many are left to grapple with the challenges of the first year of a new life without a mentor, without a plan, and without the personal care and support that every loving family should provide. I don't know about you, but I find it hard to believe that this is what God has in mind?

You know the old saying, "If it ain't broke, don't fix it." So, what would be the signs that there is a problem in the church, that something is actually broken? What about a constant increase in the number of members but the number of workers remaining the same or lukewarmness and complacency becoming the norm, would these be warning signs? Would the graying of the membership because the youth are either not being attracted to church or they're being converted but slipping through the cracks qualify?

Consider this list:

1. A revolving door, where new members come and old members drift away in equal number

2. Superficial relationships being the standard rather than the exception.

3. Few members well versed in their Bibles and sound doctrine

4. Cliques

5. Few conversions

6. Congregations that reach out almost exclusively to "their own kind"

7. An increase of immorality and blatant sin

8. Constantly growing needs with the same few people mature enough to meet them

Are these the vital signs of a healthy church? Does any of this sound familiar? Is it possible that many of our problems revolve around the way we treat our young? Leaving our children to fend in the wild is a bad strategy for any family, especially the church.

I'm glad that my mom and dad didn't abandon me (the fact that I was such a cute baby didn't hurt), and I'm equally grateful that my spiritual parents were there to mentor me during my first year as a Christian. I've been a Christian for over twenty-five years and have served as a missionary and evangelist for over twenty-three. In spite of my numerous short comings, God has used me to help great numbers of people convert, and even greater numbers of disciples mature and he has allowed me to serve in such divergent places as Nairobi, Kenya, New York, NY, Atlanta GA, and Birmingham, Al (to name a few). It's been an honor to serve. I've been blessed with being married to an amazing woman of God (my wife Michelle) for over twenty years, and I have two beautiful daughters. I know this is all from God. Left on my own, with my sinful nature, none of this would have been possible.

There's something else I know. Without John Brush, Craig Cornish, and Frazier Green, the men who took me under their wings during my first two years as a Christian, my life would have been a different story. They were there when I was most vulnerable, when my faith was new and untested. Their love and friendship was an anchor and their constant, personal biblical teaching gave me a solid scriptural foundation that I never could have acquired without their involvement. Later, when the storms came, I had a foundation, but that foundation didn't build itself. It was built brick by brick with prayer, with friendship, with sacrifice, with encouragement, with correction, and with sound, specific teaching, tailored to my struggles, my questions, and my doubts, the kind of instruction you'll never find in a new members class.

Don't get me wrong, new members classes are great and needed, and I understand that ultimately everyone is responsible for his own relationship with God, but I also understand something else. Christianity is a team sport. God designed it that way. We cannot be connected to the head, Jesus, without being connected to the body, the church (I Co 12:12-26). In fact, a major part of God's plan for his church involves us helping one another. We need strong spiritual friendships at every stage of our Christian life, but when we're young in the faith we need more than a friend. We need a mentor.

That type of mentorship is called discipling and it's something that God designed for the church.

Proverbs 13:20 *"He who walks with the wise grows wise, but a companion of fools suffers harm."*

Classes are great, and congregational fellowship is essential, but there is no substitute for the impact that one person walking with another has on the faith of a new convert. Jesus walked with the twelve, Paul walked with Timothy, and Elijah walked with Elisha. What did they know that we don't know? They knew about the power of discipling. By the end of this book, you will too.

Passing it On is designed to be a great aide to the first fifty-two weeks of a new life in Christ. The studies inside can be used for individual devotionals, but when two or three gather and study them out together, applying the scriptures, discussing the questions, confessing sin, and praying together about their resolutions, the impact of these lessons increases, exponentially. For a mature Christian looking to jumpstart your faith, Passing It On is a great refresher course to reignite the passion in your heart, for mentors, it is an invaluable tool to aide in your discipling, and for young Christians, this can be a lifeline, a lifeline to get you out of the woods and on to maturity.

Mentors Wanted

Why discipling? The church is alive. It is not a human organization or a man made structure, but the living breathing body of Christ. Christ's church is meant to be a family, not a monastery, a business, or an army; thus, everything about the body is relational. Our spirituality revolves around our bond with Christ and one another, so much of the success and failure of our journey is determined by the quality of our relationships.

With this in mind, the Holy Spirit wrote the one another commands, serving as both a road map and our lifeline. We ignore them at our peril, but when these scriptures are obeyed, we unlock the secrets of the one another way and the power of Christ's love in our fellowship. We cannot afford to fail in the restoration of these commands because so much depends on our diligence in this matter. Whether or not we realize it, the church is crying out for a revival and discipling and the one another way contain the key.

There is a loneliness in our churches, an emptiness that haunts many of our members even while they are singing in a pew, in a crowded room. Being present does not make us connected. And without true connection, we are simply familiar strangers gathered in a room, singing out of hymnals. We all want the church to be warmer, more loving, more sensitive to needs...more of a family, and at times we are simply standing around looking for someone else to fix us. The simple truth is that the secret to fixing the church requires individuals making a personal investment in one another. We need to focus on a few, pouring out our hearts, loving without limits. The spirit is waiting on us, dying to deliver us from lukewarmness, stagnation, and mediocrity. The first step toward revival involves restoration, restoration of passages and commands too long ignored. It is time we answered the question: What is discipling and how can we apply it in our church?

In English, the term discipling is not a "real" word. Disciple is not a verb. The reason why we use the term discipling is because in the original language of the New Testament, Koine Greek, disciple is used as a verb. In fact, it is used as a verb four times (Acts 14:21, Matt13:52, Matt 27:57, and Matt 28:19). Because discipling is a real Bible word, it is imperative that we define it the way the Bible does and practice it the way that the scriptures intended.

The Greek word translated to disciple is matheteuo. A more complete definition of matheteuo is: "To be or to make to be a disciple, to disciple to make a disciple to train as a follower, instruct as an adherent, to mentor. The action of the verb describes much more than academic impartation of information, it suggests the shaping of character and the cultivation of a world-view through a close, personal relationship between student and teacher" *[Definition taken from The Hebrew-Greek Key Word Study Bible page 1647].*

Matthew 28:19, the great commission, is the only one of the four verses using matheteuo which truly qualifies as a command. In this verse, we are told to go and matheteuo all nations (to train, to mold, to mentor, to disciple) and after we have discipled them, to baptize them. It is a specific command from the Lord, given to the apostles and passed on to us. The second part is like it. After the person is baptized, we are commanded to teach him to obey everything that Jesus commanded. So, Jesus commands us to disciple non-Christians in preparation for baptism and to disciple young Christians to maturity. What do we learn from this passage? We learn that discipling is biblical, it is commanded, and it is an essential aspect of our relationships with one another in God's church. Like all of God's instruction, we ignore this command at our risk, and there will be something missing from our fellowships until it is completely and accurately obeyed.

A true discipling relationship is a teacher/student relationship. It involves mentoring someone and helping to instruct and mold character. What is described here is not a peer friendship; rather, it is a relationship between an instructor and an apprentice. Discipling is a unique partnership, a specific and necessary means of accomplishing the meeting of specific needs in the church, needs that cannot be met any other way.

Even though the term matheteuo only appears in the New Testament four times, the principle can be seen throughout the Bible. It is how Moses raised up Joshua and how Elijah trained Elisha. We see it at work in the relationship of Paul and Timothy and most importantly we see that it was the method used by Jesus for molding His apostles. Discipling is certainly part of God's plan for His people. The training that God's children desperately require can only be supplied through mentorship individually and in small groups.

Help Wanted!

Ephesians 4:11-13 "*It was he who gave some to be apostles, some to be prophets, some to be evangelists, and some to be pastors and teachers, to prepare God's people for works of service, so that the body of Christ may be built up until we all reach unity in the faith and in the knowledge of the Son of God and become mature, attaining to the whole measure of the fullness of Christ."* **Verse 16** *"From him the whole body, joined and held together by every supporting ligament, grows and builds itself up in love, as each part does its work."*

II Timothy 2:2 *"And the things you have heard me say in the presence of many witnesses entrust to reliable men who will also be qualified to teach others."*

According to Ephesians 4:11-13, the primary role of the church leadership is to equip the saints for works of service. In other words, the leadership's job is to train each member how to do his job. It is not the role of the paid church leadership to go out and try to meet all the needs of the church. No individual or leadership group could accomplish this and attempting to do so will only frustrate the leaders and the church membership.

In II Timothy 2:2, Timothy, the evangelist, was instructed to entrust what he had been taught to reliable men who in turn would also be able to teach others. Jesus' plan for equipping the church involves mentoring leaders individually and in small groups and those leaders in turn mentoring others in the same fashion. This is discipling. Classes are great but without personal training, there are many lessons that Christians will never learn. Ultimately, discipleship is caught as much as it is taught. Faith is a spiritual virus passed on through contact, one heart touching another heart, one soul leading another to the foot of the cross. This is how discipling holds the key to equipping Christ's church.

On To Maturity

So, what is the goal of discipling? Maturity. What does this mean for a young Christian? A new convert who is discipled to maturity has a mastery of the basics, the ability to build and maintain spiritual friendships, and the ability to be an imitator of Jesus without being dependent on human role models. The goal is to lay a foundation and wean the student off of the need for a mentor, giving him the tools to be discipled directly from Christ through the scriptures. The goal of the mentor is to aid his pupil in acquiring the faith and insight he needs to effectively walk in Christ's steps and then once the student has those skills to get out of his way and let the focus be on Christ not man. He still needs his former teacher in his life for life, but not as a mentor walking ahead of him, but as a friend walking by his side. What is the goal of discipling? Ultimately, the goal is to disciple oneself out of a job.

Mentors Wanted

I Corinthians 11:1 *"Follow my example, as I follow the example of Christ."*

Philippians 4:9 *"Whatever you have learned or received or heard from me, or seen in me—put it into practice. And the God of peace will be with you."*

Ephesians 5:1-2 *"Be imitators of God, therefore, as dearly loved children and live a life of love, just as Christ loved us and gave himself up for us as a fragrant offering and sacrifice to God."*

In I Corinthians 11:1, Paul encouraged the Corinthian church to imitate the Jesus in him, the qualities in him that were worthy of being admired because those traits were Christ like. Much of the role of a mentor is to function as a role model, and for a pupil having one is both inspirational and serves as a practical example of biblical principles. As a young Christian, imitating the strengths of older disciples helped me to see the scriptures more clearly and gave me the faith that I too could grow in those areas. Overall, this is a good thing, for there is much all of us can learn from each other. When young in the faith, most of us are fairly dependent on the examples we see around us in the fellowship, using them as an upward call, or in the case of negative influences, allowing them to become an excuse for settling for mediocrity in our spiritual lives. Having a mentor to disciple us and be a positive influence serves as a great asset in our quest to walk in Jesus' steps and can serve to point us in the right direction. Yet, the goal of discipling is to use this influence to point the student toward Christ, not us. Human examples may point us in the right direction, but the goal is to become imitators of God (Ephesians 5:1) not man. As the student learns how to deepen his Bible study and increase his faith, he becomes less dependent on human example to flesh out the scriptures and learns to flesh them out for himself. Simply put, the mentor becomes less and Jesus becomes more.

The objective of mentoring is to lay a foundation through spiritual instruction that will allow the young Christian to go on to maturity. Maturity is not perfection and it is not reaching some superhuman standard of consistency. What we are looking for from the individuals we are helping needs to be attainable and in keeping with the scriptures. In most cases an adult convert can attain this after being disicipled a year or less although with teens and young college students, the investment is generally much longer.

I recommend five objectives to achieve in discipling a young Christian to maturity and they also serve as a way of measuring whether a disciple is reasonably mature:

5 Keys...

I. Must Possess a Sound Doctrinal Understanding of the Basics:

(Hebrews 6:1-2) According to the writer of Hebrews, there is basic theological understanding that a disciple must possess in order to be considered mature. Every disciple of Christ should have a good working knowledge of these areas so that he can progress to maturity by moving from spiritual milk to solid food. While I do not believe that Hebrews 6 is an exhaustive list, it does give us a starting point and an idea of what types of topics should be considered basics.

II. Must Be Totally Committed:

Simply put, Jesus must be Lord (Luke 9:23-26, Mt 10:32-39). In poker terms it means being all in, not perfect but 100% committed. Sometimes, we are weak, sometimes we struggle, but we must be fully committed.

III. Must Be Able to Distinguish Good from Evil (Hebrews 5:14):

He must develop the discernment to recognize sin, the conviction to deny it, and the integrity to confess and repent when he falls.

IV. Must Be Able to Initiate and Build Spiritual Friendships

A mature Christian has conviction about building and maintaining strong Proverbs 27:17, Proverbs 18:24 friendships and practicing the one another commands found throughout the scriptures.

V. Must Be Able to Study the Bible with People

The expectation is that any Christian should be able to teach someone how to become a disciple of Christ. Everyone is not going to be a Bible scholar or be the most gifted Bible teacher; yet, one does not need to be in order to show someone from the scriptures how to have a relationship with God. In Matthew 9:36-38, Jesus looked at the harvest of souls before Him and lamented that the workers are few. As we disciple, we multiply workers because by the time someone has been discipled to maturity, he should be a productive worker for the Lord.

To help young Christians with their growth, when each is converted, a mature Christian or group of Christians should volunteer to disciple him/her. In addition to loving their new brother or sister and sharing their lives with him or her, the mentors should commit to studying the Bible with the new member once a week, investing time and helping their student to learn the fundamentals. This mentor should not be the young converts only relationship, but this individual is the one who has accepted the responsibility for personal training and instruction. In my experience, if we invest in people, a foundation can be laid in months not years, but if we do not invest, disciples can be around for decades and never mature. When the time is right, the mentorship concludes, but the friendship continues for a lifetime.

Sermons and classes are useful, but by themselves, they can never replace the personal touch. Passing it on, one soul touching another, is how we are going to grow the church and evangelize the world. We have everything we need to realize Jesus' plan. We have the word, we have the Holy Spirit, and if we are active in sharing our faith, we have people getting converted. We just need to add one more crucial ingredient:

Mentors willing to share not only the gospel but their lives as well (I Thessalonians 2:8). There is no role more rewarding and few that can equal its importance.

Practical Discipling

The two men who had the biggest impact on my Christian walk, during the first year of my new life, were John Brush and Craig Cornish (I met Frazier Green in year two). I thank God for them and the way they sacrificed their time for me. This may be hard to believe, but rumor has it that I can be a little difficult. Well, back then, I was totally out of control, fresh out of the world, a cocky, arrogant, insecure kid with daddy issues. I constantly tested those two and never tried to let on how much I respected and needed their friendship, but they did far more than just put up with me. They opened wide their hearts, and helped me see Jesus. My life was forever changed.

Like me, Craig was a student at the University of Maryland. Craig was the one who walked with me constantly, teaching me the nuts and bolts of the Christian life. Much of what I learned was caught. I got to hang out with him and see his faith in action, his commitment to purity, and his colorblind love for the saints and the lost. Many other things he taught me directly, pulling me aside to teach me important lessons, and to use scripture to offer correction when necessary (with me that was fairly often). God chose the perfect mentor for me. He was patient, humble, gentle, persistent, and even keeled, my exact opposite. By imitating the Jesus in him, I became a better man.

John was our campus minister, and he was a great friend as well. He was married with two twin toddlers, so he was not nearly as available as Craig. Still, every week he made time to get with me. He'd talk to me about how I was doing and what I was feeling, and he would study the Bible with me, giving me books to read and scriptures to study in-between our sessions. From John, I learned how to truly study the Bible, not simply reading words on a page, but practically applying the scriptures to my life and using them as my standard in every situation. He showed concern for me in our talks, listening to my fears, my doubts, my sins, and even my crazy dreams, and then every week, he would show me the answers to my questions in God's word. The power of our times is not that he fed me with the word. What John did was so much more powerful than that. He taught me how to feed myself.

This is the essence of discipling, walking with someone daily and sitting down to teach the scriptures regularly. If we simply hang out and never open the Bible, our relationships will be worldly or human focused. If we only study the word together without sharing our lives, the impact will be theoretical and superficial. True mentorship requires both.

Look, I understand that we're not all college students. As we get older, life gets more complicated and time gets scarcer. How can we as mentors walk with someone daily, even if we are paired up with another mentor for help? By being creative. We live during a time where God has equipped us with a variety of ways to stay in touch. The phone is our friend in this matter. If we're creative and committed to our relationships, we will make a way.

The remainder of this book is fifty-two Bible studies. As stated earlier, these studies are equally helpful for mature or young Christians. They can be used for devotional times and be very effective. While this is true, for those interested in discipling the young, these lessons are at their best when used as mentoring studies, designed to help disciple a new convert to maturity.

I would suggest both mentor and student getting a copy of the book and having the baby Christian study the scriptures in each lesson throughout the week for his devotional times during the week preceding the sessions. During the sessions the mentor can go through the study with his friend helping him to apply it practically for his life and his situations. The lessons will help build a biblical foundation, and it will also work to create opportunities for open and honest dialogue. Those conversations will knit your hearts together as you walk side by side down the narrow road.

Oh, before you get started, you may want to review the following areas with the new convert and study them out if needed.

1. Biblical conversion
2. The Gifts of the Holy Spirit
3. Specific False Doctrines

Together, let's pass it on. Enjoy! And may God bless you.

In Him,

F. Barton Davis

(If you are interested in learning more about discipling and Christian friendships, you'll find my book <u>Closer Than a Brother</u> helpful.) www.magimediapub.com

Recommended Reading

These are few books that every young Christian should read. **Enjoy!**

1. **Thirty Days At the Foot of the Cross**   Thomas and Shelia Jones

2. **A Tale of Three Kings**   Gene Edwards

3. **The Disciplined Life**   Richard S. Taylor

4. **Closer Than a Brother**   F. Barton Davis

5. **Will the Real Heretics Please Stand Up**   David W. Berot

6. **The ABC's of Grace**   Jack Exum

7. **True & Reasonable**   Douglas Jacoby

8. **Mere Christianity**   C.S. Lewis

9. **Prepared to Answer: Confronting Religious Doctrines With Biblical Teaching**   Gordon Ferguson

10. **More Than a Carpenter**   Josh D. McDowell & Sean McDowell

11. **The Master Plan of Evangelism**   Robert E. Coleman

12. **The Lion Never Sleeps**   Mike Taliaferro

Christian Fiction

1. **Shadow Dancers** by F. Barton Davis
2. **The Screw Tape Letters**   C.S. Lewis
3. **This Present Darkness** Frank Peritti

To Order Go to:

www.magimediapub.com

God Is Right

Intro:
One of the most challenging aspects of being a Christian is obeying the word even when what is said is hard to obey or difficult to accept. It's a major shift because we have had a lifetime of living according to our feelings, our judgments, and our understanding. Compounding the problem is the fact that the Bible will often contradict what our family has taught us, what the world endorses, and even our own religious traditions. We have to constantly remind ourselves that God is right and to daily allow the word to stir our hearts and lead us back to Jesus. Here are some good reminders.

God is Omniscient

He's all knowing. Think about that. What does that mean? In part, it means...

1. He knows our past. (**Psalm 39:4, Psalm 139: 1-18**)
2. He knows our future. (Psalm 39:4, Psalm 139: 1-18)
3. He's numbered our days, every hair on our head.(Psalm 139:16)
4. He knows our hearts **John 21: 17, Proverbs 16:2, 16:25** (He knows our deeds, both good and bad...but he knows and weighs our motives...we don't always know our motives...that's why we need the word **James 1:22-23, Hebrews 4:12-13**
5. He knows what's best for us Proverbs 16:2, 16:25
6. He knows every mystery (When you get a chance, please read **Job chapters 38 & 39**...God knows the dimensions of the heavens, etc.)
7. He Knows What We Need to Know **Deuteronomy 29:29**. (God doesn't reveal everything, but reveals everything we need to know)

He's Always Right

(Psalm 19: 1-4, 7-11, Psalm 119:9-10, 127-128)

1. He's right even when it doesn't feel right.
Questions:
   a. What are some truths from the Bible that are difficult to accept?
   b. What are some areas where the Bible's teaching is different than what your family has taught you? How does that make you feel?
   c. When the Bible says something different form "the experts" who's right? (examples: Homosexuality, divorce, abortion, premarital sex, lust, masturbation, etc.)
   d. What about if the word says something different than what popular Christian leaders teach?   Who's right? How does that make you feel?
   e. Why is it so important to read the Bible daily?
   f. When you feel one way but the Bible is telling you something else, what should you do?

A Few Additional Scriptures:
   1. (Psalm 119: 137-142, 127-128, 105-107, 89-92, 71-72, 9-10)
   2. Galatians 1:6-10
   3. Isaiah 55: 9-10
   4. Proverbs 30:5-6
   5. Acts 4:8-22

Important Study Aides:

1. Concordances (allows you to look up every use of a particular word)
2. Commentaries & Study Bibles (Great resources but remember the commentary is written by men not God)
3. A Great Book on the Topic: <u>True & Reasonable</u> Douglas Jacoby
4. <u>Mere Christianity</u> by C.S. Lewis
5. Helpful sites:
   a. www.studylight.org
   b. www.biblestudytools.com
   c. www.biblegateway.com

God Has a People

Intro: **I Peter 2:9-12:** God has a people. It is Christ's Body, Christ's people, Christ's Church **(Colossians 1:1-18).** It is the prayer of our Lord that His people are united **(John 17:20-23).** Christians need to remember what unites us, defines us and makes us special.

Blood Is Our Passport

(Acts 26:27-28, John 3:1-7, Acts 2:38, I John 5:8 Romans 6:1-7)
Our forgiveness through Christ's blood is what defines us. Question: Since that is the case, should congregations be divided over race?   Class?   Politics? Personality?   How does this division make Christ feel?

Love Is Our Language

(John 13:34-35, I Co 13:1-8, 13)
Questions?
1. What is the standard of love we should have for each other?
2. How is this different from ordinary love?
3. How important is it to God that we display this type of love? What are some practical ways we can demonstrate this?
4. What are some areas where your love needs to grow?

Faith Is Our Culture

(II Co 5:7, Hebrews 11:1-6)
Questions:
1. What is the hardest part of living by faith?
2. Why is it so important?

Heaven Is Our Home

(I Peter 2: 11-12)

Ties into Hope in verse (I Co 13.13). This world is not our home. This is not our comfort, not our reward, only a means to a greater end.

God Is Love

Intro: God is love **(I John 4:7-21).** What is Grace? It is often defined as unmerited favor, but another way of thinking of it is that grace is the practical manifestation of God's love.

Grace is Free

What is grace? (Greek Charis: from its root, that which causes joy **[Taken from the Keyword Study Bible].** In reference to God it is the absolutely free expression of His loving kindness toward us. **Isaiah 26:10, John 1:16, Romans 1:20**
Grace is the essence of God's divine nature. God's grace comes in many different forms. It is the practical manifestation of God's love. It is not just centered on salvation (although the gift of salvation is the ultimate testimony to God's grace). Still, it just didn't start there because we all benefited from God's grace even when we were lost. Every breath we've taken, bite of food we've eaten, and door that's been opened has been God's grace in action, given freely to all **Matthew 5:45.**

Question:
1. What are some examples of God's grace in your life?
2. How does it make you feel knowing that God's love has always been working on your behalf during your life?
3. Can God's discipline be an act of Grace? Why? Why not?
4. How have you seen this in your life?

Grace Is Conditional (Ephesians 2:8-10)

God loves everyone, but does that mean that everyone is saved? People get confused about the topic of grace because they confuse general references to God's grace with specific references to grace as it works in relation to salvation. In pertaining to sin, grace could only come through atonement. Grace had a price (Jesus death) and in reference to forgiveness it has conditions. It's a free gift not a free ride. As it pertains to salvation, there are conditions for receiving God's forgiveness {**Romans 3: 21-26** (faith), **Luke 13:1-5, Luke 17: 3-4, Romans 2:5, Matthew 6: 14-15, Jonah 2: 8** (repentance), **Romans 6:1-7** (baptism), **Luke 9:23, Luke 14:25** (Whole heartedness), etc.}, and there are conditions for staying in God's grace (**I John 1: 6-7, Colossians 1: 21-23, Hebrews 10:26-31**). It's impossible to earn salvation. Nothing we can ever do is equal to the gift being given, but obeying conditions is not the same as working for salvation. For example: If I won 100 million dollars in the lottery, I would have to follow some procedures to collect the money. The Gift is free (I didn't earn it), but I would still have to follow the procedures to procure it. If I refused to obey, I could never collect my gift. Salvation is the same way. We'll never be perfect and we'll never be worthy, but we still have to obey God's plan for salvation in order to receive the gift. Those who do not faithfully respond to God's plan will remain in their sins.

Questions:
1. If Grace is a free gift, does it matter what you believe? Does it matter how you live? Why?

Grace Is Unfair:

It's not fair. **(Isaiah 1:18-19, Romans 6: 23) We deserve death!** It is not fair that Jesus died in our place. What is fair is for us to die for our sins. Grace is unfair to our advantage. God accepts our best even though our best isn't good enough. Jesus makes up the difference!

God Is Love II

Intro: I have exciting news. I'm perfect, blameless, and totally free from sin. In fact I'm not guilty of any sin.

Question:
How do you feel about that statement? Do you think that it is true?

We Are Perfect or We are Lost! (Colossians 1:13-14, 21-24)

What it means to be saved is to be perfect, but the perfection is not achieved by our performance, far from it. In Christ, our sins are washed away. We stand before God without stain or blemish. As we continue to walk in the light, Christ's blood continually cleanses us. But we must remain in Him. God won't leave us but we can leave Him (**Hebrews 10:26-31, Hebrews 6:4-6).** Outside of Christ, **Isaiah 59:1-3** is our reality. In Christ, **Isaiah 1:18-19** is our reality. **In Christ,** we should have confidence. Satan does not want us to know that we are perfect. This is who we really are. **James 5:16**…our prayers are powerful. Why? Because we are righteous. Jesus makes us so, God's love in action.

Questions
    1. Should we feel insecure about our salvation?
    2. Does this mean that I can sin as much as I like?

We Must Walk In the Light (Colossians 1:23, I John 1:5-10)

What is the condition for remaining perfect through Christ's blood. We must remain in Christ, in other words, walk in the light.

A. **Walking In the Light is About Commitment Not Perfection**: God does not require that we are sinless, but he requires that we make every effort to be righteous **(Luke 9:23-26, Mark 12:28-31, Luke 14:25-27, Luke 13:22-25)**. Even our best effort falls short, but he requires that we give 100% effort. 99% won't do. We do our best and Jesus fills in the rest. He makes up the difference, but he does not tolerate us holding back.

B. **We Must Live a Lifestyle of Repentance:** Yes we sin but we cannot have a casual attitude about it. When we fall we need to confess our sins and make a decision to repent.. **(Acts 3:19, James 5:16, Matthew 5:27-30)**

C. **Never Give Up (Acts 14:21-22):** We will go through hard times. Don't quit. We can choose to leave the light, but if we remain in Him, Jesus will pull us through.

Questions:
1. How does this make you feel?
2. What's the best part of being in the light?
3. What's the hardest part?
4. Is there anything that you need to confess?
5. Why is it important to confess?
6. Why is it important to share our faith?

God Is Our Father

You've heard the commercial, a few years ago, which asked the question. "Is it in you?" Well, if you are a Christian, **GOD IS IN YOU.**

We Have His DNA (I Co 6:9-11, 12-20, Romans 8:5-17, Ephesians 1:11-14, 18-20)

We have God himself dwelling inside of us, His spirit, His power, His spiritual DNA:

1. Gives us power to overcome our sinful nature. We have the power
2. It is a deposit that proves that we are his children. His spiritual DNA lives in us.
3. The Spirit gives us the power to overcome **(Romans 8:31-39).**
4. Our actions affect His spirit (we can grieve the spirit **Ephesians 4:30**, we can put out the spirit's fire **I Thessalonians 5:19**, and we should make every effort to keeping in step with the spirit **Galatians 5:25.**)
5. Our Father hears us and answers us. **(I John 5:13-15, James 5:17-18)**

Questions:
1. What type of confidence should we have in overcoming sin? Difficult circumstances?
2. What kind of confidence should we have in our prayer life?
3. Since God is our Father, how does He feel about us? Should we ever question His love for us?
4. What makes you insecure about your relationship with God? Should you be? Why? Why not?

God Is Fearsome & Compassionate

Intro: (**Hebrews 13:8**) We've got to be sure that we truly know the God of the Bible. Frankly, sometimes the Bible's picture of God is confusing…

God Is Compassionate

> *God Is Love: **I John 4: 7-12, 16**
> **Unimaginable Love: **Ephesians 3: 16-19**
> ***God Is **I Co Chapter 13**
> ****He wipes every tear from our eyes: **Rev. 21:1-5**

God Is Fearsome

> *God has done terrifying things **II Peter: 4-10:** He does them still, and will do so again with no apologies
> **It is a dreadful thing to fall into His hands: **Hebrews 10: 26-31**
> ***Punishes severely: **Exodus 20: 4-5**
> ****He will Burn the unsaved forever: **Revelation 21: 6-8**

To have a mature faith, we need to reconcile these two aspects of God's character. If we just focus on God's compassion, we tend to tolerate sin, embrace cheap grace, practice worldly repentance, and have an ungrateful spirit. If we only focus on God's fearsome nature, we tend to be legalistic in our thinking, always feel guilty, attempt to work our way to heaven, and be insecure of our salvation. God is not one or the other but both and our view of Him should reflect this reality. How does it work?

It's All About Noah and the Ark (Genesis 6:6-8, Genesis 6:9-22, 6: 11-16, 7:13-24)

The story of Noah is a key. If we understand it, we'll have greater understanding of God's character: Because of sin God destroyed the world, sparing only eight people. Everyone Noah knew drowned before his eyes. In all probability, Noah's grandfather, Methuselah, the oldest man in the Bible died in the flood (we know for a fact that he died the year of the flood **Gen 5:25-31, 7:11**). When Noah looked over the side of the ark, he saw horrifying sights, the physical evidence of God's wrath, but when he saw the ark, he saw tangible proof of God's compassion. Everyone on the ark experienced nothing but God's saving grace, only seeing the vengeful side of God from a distance, protected by the safety of the ark. I'm sure Noah and his family experienced conflicting emotions. They were terrified at the carnage surrounding them, but they also felt special, loved, and undeserving that God chose them to be the remnant saved from a condemned world.. Here's the thing though, Noah's story is our story.

1. Like Noah, our world has been sentenced for destruction **II Peter 3: 3-13**
2. Jesus Is our Ark **(John 14:6):** Just as 8 souls were saved by Noah's ark, only those who find Jesus and remain in Him will be saved from the coming wrath.
3. Everyone who remains in our ark (Jesus) will only experience God's grace and mercy. Everyone outside of the ark will only see God's judgment.
4. Our mission is to bring as many people into the ark as possible.

Questions:

1. How do you think Noah felt as he witnessed the flood? How would you have felt?
2. If you were on the ark during the flood, do you think you'd play near the ledge to see how close you could get to falling without falling off? How does this apply to us in our Christian walk?
3. What are some ways that we can play near the edge?
4. Unlike Noah we have the chance to rescue people? What should our attitude be about that? How is it going for you?

God Is Holy

Intro: God Is Holy. What does that mean?

Leviticus 22:32: There are several Hebrew words for holy:
Qados – [Exodus 19:6, Leviticus 19:2, 20:7, 20:8. 20:26, etc...]
It means consecrated, sacred, pure, holy... essentially denotes
what is intrinsically sacred and distinct...In relationship with
God, God is separate from all evil, cannot tolerate sin, His
majestic holiness is without equal and is completely perfect.
Qadas – [Gen. 2:3, Exodus 29:37, 31:13, Leviticus 22:32,
etc...] To be clean, to pronounce clean, to sanctify, to
purify...denotes being pure or devoted to God. Signifies an act
or state in which people or things are set aside and reserved
exclusively for God. **Qodes** – [Exodus 3:5, 15:13, Leviticus
10:10,etc...]To Consecrate. Holiness, the most holy
thing...something consecrated to God.

Two of the words translated holy in the New Testament are:
Hagiazo – Devoted to God, holy, sacred. The fundamental idea
is separation from ordinary or common usage and devotion to
divine usage: **Haigos** – Something holy is that which has been
brought into a relationship with God and designated by Him
having a sacred purpose.)[**Definitions taken from the Key
Word Study Bible**]

God Is Holy, blameless, spotless, and perfect. **I John 1:5** tells
us that God is Light. In Him there is no darkness at all. When
we are set apart by God we become what He is. We take on His
characteristics. God Is Holy. There is no one, nothing like
Him. Here's the challenge, he calls us to be holy as well.
**Leviticus 11:44, 11:45, 19:1-2, Hebrews 12:14-17, I Peter
1:13-16. What does this mean?**

We Have Been Set Apart (I Co 6:9-20)

1. We are one with Christ
2. We are the temple for the Holy Spirit
4. Christ makes us holy

We Have Been Called to a Higher Standard

(Ephesians 5:1-14)
1. We are called to imitate God
2. Called to have not even a hint of sin
    a. What does this mean?
    b.   What are some examples of a hint?
    c. How does it affect the places that we go? The music that we listen to? The movies we watch? Etc.
3. We are called to be radical in our repentance **(Matthew 5:27-30)**

Questions:
1. Is God the standard of your righteousness or is it the world?
2. Does Matthew 5:27-30 describe your attitude about sin?

God Is Jealous

Intro:
Have you ever known someone jealous? How'd they act?

God is Jealous

Exodus 34:14: God whose name is jealous. It's about exclusive devotion. He will tolerate no rivals. This is His nature. **Exodus 20:5**,Additional scriptures: DT 5:9, DT 6:13-19, DT 32:16, Psalm 78:58, Psalm 79:5 Ezekiel 16:38, Nahum 1:2 […The Lord is a jealous and avenging God], I Co 10:22. God's Jealousy is a hard teaching.

No Rivals (DT 4: 21-24)

He must be the only one we worship

Questions
1. Today, what are some things people worship
2. How does that make God feel?

Lordship is the Standard

1. Lordship is the cost of having a relationship with God **(Luke 10:27, Luke 14: 25-27, Luke 9:23-26)**
2. Lordship is about total surrender **(Luke 9:57-62)**
3. It's a relationship and God wants all or nothing at all.

Questions:
1. What rivals your love for God?
2. How does God feel about half-hearted commitment?
3. What is the hardest thing for you to surrender?

Additional reading: Mark 10:17-31

Because He Rose

Intro: John 3:16 We know value by the price someone is willing to pay. What was the price Jesus paid for us?

The Cross Will Show You What your Worth (Isaiah 52:13-15, 53:1-6)

Questions:

1. How would you describe Christ's suffering on the cross?
2. He took on our sin? What was your part in Christ's suffering?
3. Jesus went thorough so much for you. Why?
4. Do you ever wonder about your worth, your value?
5. What does the cross say about how much Jesus values you?

The Empty Tomb Will Give You Hope (John 20:1-18)

Questions:
1. How would you have reacted if you found the empty tomb?
2. What kind of power does it take to perform that miracle? What kind of power lives in us? **(Ephesians 1:18-20)**
3. How does that make you feel?

Because He Rose

Because He rose, I will rise
Because He lives, I can live
Because he won, I will win, despite the odds, despite the facts
I will rise, I will win, I will dream.
Because He rose.

Because He rose, I will preach and I will never stop
Do you know what I know? Sees what I see?
Come and see the empty tomb that set this captive free.
And I am free, truly free
Because He rose

At the foot of the cross I see my sin.
At the foot of the cross I see His grace
At the foot of the cross I see the cost
At the foot of the cross I kneel in place.
In the empty tomb I get a second chance.
And I will take the chance and dream great dreams
Because He rose.
Because He Rose.

The Miracle of Prayer

Intro: Luke 11:1-4 Prayer is God's gift to us.

Make Prayer a Priority

1. Jesus made prayer a priority **(Mark 1:35-36, Luke 6:12-16)**
2. We need to pray on all occasions **(I Thessalonians 5:16-17, Ephesians 6:18-20)**
3. The word is how God speaks to us and prayer is how we speak to God. We need to have daily conversations with God **(Ephesians 6:17).**

We Need to Pray With Faith

1. We must not doubt **(James 1:5-8)**
2. We must be persistent **Luke 11:5-13**

We Must Pray From the Heart

1. Open Up to God **(I Samuel 1:9-20)**
2. No topic is off limits
3. He wants us to be vulnerable **(read through the Psalms. Some examples: Psalm 73, Psalm 51, Psalm 42,Psalm 27, etc.) We need to imitate their vulnerability.**

Questions:

1. How is your prayer life?
2. Are you spending consistent quality time?
3. Are you being vulnerable in your prayers?
4. Are you praying with faith?

Advice

Intro: Seeking advice from spiritual people is important to being a disciple of Christ and one of the keys to being wise. Advice is not scripture. When it comes to scripture, God doesn't advise. He commands. Advice is not permission. The final decision rests with the person getting the advice. Yet, it is part of God's process for making spiritual decisions. Often, God uses people to show us his will and to point us in the right direction.

1. Proverbs 11:14
2. Proverbs 12:15
3. Proverbs 13:10
4. Proverbs 13:20
5. Proverbs 14:12
6. Proverbs 15:12
7. Proverbs 15:22
8. Proverbs 18:13
9. Proverbs 20:18
10. Proverbs 24:6
11. Proverbs 28:26

Advice is a Choice

Proverbs 23:9 also Proverbs 9:7-9   You cannot make someone take advice, and shouldn't give advice to someone you know doesn't want it. Don't ask for advice if all you want is approval! Advice is about wisdom and foolishness. People have the right to be foolish! It isn't wise but it is our choice.

Great Illustration of this: Read 2 Kings 12: 1-17

1. Who was Rehoboam?

2. Did Rehoboam want advice or approval?
3. Why did he ignore the men who had advised the world's wisest man, his father, Solomon?
4. What was the result of Rehoboam's decision?
5. What are some things we can learn from his example?
6. What do you think are some areas where you need to seek advice from spiritual people?
7. How can we identify who would be good to ask? (Answer: people who are mature, spiritual and have positive experience in the area where you are seeking help)

Another Example Acts 16: 1-3

There was no biblical command for Christians to be circumcised, so Paul had no authority to command Timothy to go through circumcision (it is very painful as an adult). Paul believed that being circumcised would make Timothy more effective as a missionary so he advised Timothy to get one.

1. Did Timothy have a choice?
2. Why do you think he listened to Paul?
3. How does this apply to us?

Before you get advice, always ask yourself if you want advice or approval. Do you want wisdom or do you just want someone to agree? There's a difference.   When you want advice, you seek out the most spiritual, the most knowledgeable advisers, and you want to hear what they have to say whether it agrees with your view or not. You need to be willing to sincerely listen and consider what is being said.   If more than one spiritual person is giving you the same advice, it should mean something. Maybe, God is talking to you. When you want approval, you want people to scratch your itching ears. You seek out "advisers' you know will side with you. It's your choice, and at the end of the day, we have to take responsibility for our spiritual lives (**Philippians 2: 12**). Advice is simply a tool that God gives us. Used correctly it can help us be wise

Resolving Conflict & Unity

Intro: (John 17:20-23, Romans 12:16-18, James 4:1-12) To Have unity we must learn to biblically resolve conflict.

God Expects Us to Resolve Conflict **(Philippians 4:2-3)**
1. We are to tell the truth to each other, even when it is difficult **(Proverbs 27:5-6, Proverbs 28:23, Ephesians 4:14-16)**
2. God expects us to fight for unity **(Ephesians 4:2-3)**
3. God expects us to forgive **(Colossians 3:13-14)**
4. Forgiveness is unilateral. We forgive because Christ forgave us. We need to forgive the act, even if the offender has not yet repented. It is impossible to resolve conflict before we have forgiven **(Mt 18:21-35, I Peter4:8)**

Questions:

1. Is it OK to not be completely honest with each other in order to avoid conflict? Why? Why not?
2. Why is it so important to be honest when we have a concern about a brother or sister?
3. Does it matter how we communicate? How should we communicate?
4. Is possible to resolve conflict if we have not forgiven from the heart?

God Gives Us a Plan (Mt 18:15-17, I Co 6:1-8)

1. What is God's plan to resolve conflict between disciples?
2. Is it OK to talk to others before we've gone directly to the person?
3. Why is it important to go to the person first?
4. What is the next step?
5. Why is it important to go together to meet with others?
6. What is the meaning of **(I Co 6:7)?** How does it relate to resolving conflict?
7. Do you have unresolved conflict in your life?
8. Have you followed God's plan to resolve it?

The Kingdom of God

Intro: What is the Kingdom of God?

1. God's eternal Kingdom coming to earth was prophesied **(Daniel 2: 1-23, Daniel 2: 24-49, Isaiah 2:1-4, Mt 3:1-2, Mt 4:17)**
2. The Kingdom of God was predicted to come with power **(Mark 9:1. Luke 24:45-49)**
3. The way into the Kingdom is being born again **(John 3:1-5)**
4. The Kingdom of God came during the lifetime of the apostles on the day of Pentecost shortly after Jesus resurrection **(Mark 9:1, Acts 2:1-12).**
5. The Kingdom of God on earth is God's church **(Mt 16:13-19)**

What does this mean for us?

The Church is not a Building (Matthew 16:13-19)

1. The church is the people not a building. We are the people who have built their faith in the rock, the foundation, Jesus. **(Mt 16:18, I Co 3:10-11)**
2. The church is not a man made organization but the Kingdom of God on earth.

God's Church is the Winning Team

1. The Gates of Hell will not prevail **(Mt 16:18)**
2. We have already won **(Revelation 12:7-12)**

We Must Seek the Kingdom First (Matthew 6:19-24, 25-33)

1. The Kingdom must be our treasure
2. Pleasing God and serving His Kingdom must be our first priority

Questions:

1. How do we practically seek first the Kingdom?
2. What are some obstacles to it?

Commitment to the Body

Intro: The church is the body of Christ **(Ephesians 1:22-23, Ephesians 4:4-6, Ephesians 4:11-16, Ephesians 4: 25-27, I Co 6:12-20)**

What this Means...

We Must Be Devoted to Each Other (Acts 2:42-47)

What is devoted? **Greek: Proskartereo** (to endure, to remain somewhere, to remain steadfastly with someone, to stick faithfully with someone...referring to those who insist on something or stay close to someone. **[Definition taken from the Keyword Study Bible]**

Questions:

1. What are the things to which they were devoted?
2. What does it mean to be devoted to the fellowship?
3. Can you be devoted if you do not consistently attend?

How devoted is devoted? (Hebrews 10:23-25, Hebrews 10:32-34)

Questions:

1. What kind of persecution had the church been through?
2. In this passage, what was the expectation concerning commitment to assembling?
3. What should it be for us?
4. Has this been your standard of devotion?

We Must Be Connected. (I Co 12:12-26)

1. You need the body 21-22. None of us can survive spiritually without being connected to God's people)
2. The body needs you. (18-20). We all play an important role. There are things that only you can do, needs only you can meet.
3. Let's replace criticism with involvement
4. Serving God must be our first priority **(Mt 6:33)**

Questions:

1. What are some ways we can be connected to the body?
2. Are you connected and involved?
3. Is serving God your first priority?

A Powerful Delusion

Intro: (II Thessalonians 2:9-12) Beware of false doctrine. Among other things, this passage teaches if we do not love the truth (God's word), we will be led astray.

What Is False Doctrine?

1. (Revelation 22:18-20, Deuteronomy 4:2, Proverbs 30:6) False doctrine is adding or subtracting from God's word
2. (Galatians 1:6-10) No matter how credible the teacher, if his teaching is different than what the Bible teaches, it is false doctrine and it is dangerous.
3. (Mark 7:1-8, Mt 15:1-20) We cannot put our confidence in religious tradition. We must test our traditions and beliefs against God's word.

We Can Be Sincere and Still Be Sincerely Wrong

1. **(Mt 7:21-23, 24-27)** Sincere faith in false doctrine will not save you
2. **(I Kings 13)** Sincerity does not replace obedience
3. **(I Tim 4:1-5)** False teaching is dangerous

How Should We Feel About It?

1. **(I Co 15:33-34)** We should be careful about our fellowship.
2. **(Mt 16:5-12)** We should guard our hearts against it.

Questions:

1. If we believe in Jesus and try to be good people, is our doctrine important?
2. Does it matter where we go to church? Why? Why not?
3. How important is it for us to read our Bible and know what it says?
4. How important is it for us to share our faith?

One True Church

Intro: (Important! Your homework before doing this study is to study out the conversions in the book of Acts.)
Question: There are many denominations. Does God only have one true church?

What Does the Bible Teach?

    A. **Ephesians 1:22-23, Ephesians 4:4-6, Colossians 1:17-18**: The body is the church. There is only one body. **There is only one church.**

    B. The church is part of God's eternal kingdom **Matthew 16:13-19**

    C. The church is God's not ours: **Colossians 1: 17-18, Romans 16:16**. Only one head, Jesus. He gives us His word to direct us. No man or group of men has authority to add or subtract from God's word **(Rev 22:18-20)**. All who truly belong to Jesus are part of His church. Ultimately, only He knows the membership. Local congregations who are faithful to His message are part of His one true church.

Things We Need to Know

    I.   **There Is Only One Way In** (Review Conversions in Acts)

    II.   **There Is Only One Foundation (Ephesians 2:19-22, Ephesians 4:4-6, Hebrews 5: 11-6:3)**

        A. If the cornerstones of the faith are not in tact, it is a counterfeit church.

        B. Jesus and His word must be the final authority. No other head

III.   A Congregation Can Lose its Lamp Stand

    A. (Revelation 2:4-5, 2:12-16, 2:18-25, 3:1-6, 3:14-22)

    B. We must protect our life & doctrine **(I Tim 4:15-16, John 4:24)**

IV.   God's True Church Is for All People (Mt 28:18-20, Isaiah 2:1-5, Colossians 3:11-14)

Questions:

1. What did you learn when you studied out the conversions in Acts? Should our conversions differ from theirs? Why? Why not?
2. What are some ways we can protect our life and doctrine?
3. How can we tell if we are in a counterfeit church? What should we do?

I am a member of Christ's Church

It is not an organization. It is not a corporation. It is not a building.

It is not divided. It is not confused. It is not segregated

Its head is not an evangelist, not an elder, or a board member.

It is a living, breathing, organism,

Led by Christ and belonging to God.

I am a member of Christ's Church

It was not founded by human decision

It will not end by human will

Man cannot change it, update it, or improve it.

It was purchased with blood and it began with power.

It cannot has not and never will be shaken

And the gates of hell cannot prevail against it.

There is only one church in this city

There is only one church in this country,

There is only one church in this world

And I am a member.

The way is narrow

Man did not let me in and man cannot put me out

I am a member of the Christ's Church

 It is more than a name on a building

It is more than a local congregation

It is God's eternal kingdom

I am a member of the Christ's Church

His vision; His mission; His way,
And I will serve it 'til death and beyond.

We are His church. We are God's people.
Since we are the body, let us walk as Jesus did

Repentance

Intro: **What does it truly mean to repent?**

Read: (II Co 7:8-11, Matthew 5:27-30, Acts 26:20)

Questions:

1. How do these passages define repentance? Is it more than just feeling sorry about my sins?
2. From II Co 7:8-11, what is the difference between worldly sorrow and Godly sorrow?
3. Where does worldly sorrow lead? Why?
4. Where does Godly sorrow lead? Why?
5. Can you tell when someone has repented? How?
6. **What are some things from which you've repented?**

Read: (Acts 3:19, Luke 13:1-5, Psalm 38:1-10)

Questions:

1. Can we be forgiven of sin if we do not repent? Why? Why not?
2. How did un-repented sin make David feel in Psalm 38? Have you ever felt this way?
3. What promises does God make in Acts 3:19?
4. What are some ways that repentance brings on God's refreshment?
5. What are the areas in your life where you need to repent of sin? How can I help?

Suggested Reading: Repentance by Ed Anton

Getting to the Root

Intro: Have you ever done gardening or yard work? What is the only way to really kill a weed? Answer: You've got to destroy the roots. In the same way we need to get to the root sins in our sinful nature. All of us fall short in many ways, but we all have some root sins that manifest in different ways at different times of our lives. They can have many different branches (example: the root sin of pride can cause deceit, anger, greed, jealousy, envy, etc.). The roots aren't necessarily the sins that others readily see, but they tend to be the sins of the heart that get the ball rolling. **Read I Samuel 11,** for example #2: King David's pride led to complacency, led to lust, led to adultery, led to deceit, and finally murder.

Read: (Galatians 5:19-21, II Tim 3:1-7)

Questions:

1. Compare the sin list from Galatians 5 with the one in II Timothy. What's the primary difference? Is one list worse than the other? Why? Why not?
2. What are some root sins that you see in II Tim 3:1-7. What are some of the branches that these sins can sprout?
3. When you look at your life, are there root sins that have been at work, manifesting in different ways? What do you think they are?
4. What are some things that you can do to be on guard against these sins?

Christian Dating

Intro: Dating did not exist in biblical times. But God gave us principles that we can use to guide every aspect our lives, dating included. When speaking of dating, this study is referring to romantic dating, serious relationships

We Can Learn Much From Relationships in the Old Testament (Romans 15:4)

1. The things written in the Old Testament were written to teach us **(Romans 15:4)**
2. During Old Testament times, God set His chosen people apart and did not allow them to marry followers of false gods. **(Ezra 9:1-4, Ezra 10:1-16, Nehemiah 13:23-28)**
3. In the New Testament, God only permits Christians to marry Christians **(I Co 7:39-40)**

Questions:

1. Since **(Ezra 9:1-4, Ezra 10:1-16, Nehemiah 13:23-28)** were written to teach us, what lessons does God want us to learn form these passages?
2. In light of these passages, do you think God has an opinion about Christians who date outside of their faith? How do you think God feels?
3. If Christians are supposed to marry Christians, does it make sense for them to date non-Christians? Why? Why not?

We Must Not Date the World (II Corinthians 6:14-18)

1. What does it mean when oxen are evenly yoked? What happens if they are uneven?
2. Why is it important for Christians to be evenly yoked?

3. What are some examples of people being yoked? What if two people are in love, does that qualify? Why? Why not?
4. **(I Co 15:33-34)** Who is the bad company in this passage? Why are people who believe false doctrines considered bad company? Does this apply to dating? Why? Why not?
5. If a Christian dates someone who is unsaved, is he evenly yoked? Does it make God happy?

We Must Not Date Like the World

1. **(I Timothy 5:1-2)** We need to treat each other as sisters and brothers, with absolute purity.
2. We need to dress modestly **(I Tim 2:9-10, Mark 9:42-48)**
3. **(Ephesians 5:3)** There must not even be a hint of sexual immorality on your dates.

Trust God

1. **(Psalm 37:1-5)** Trust God. Wait on Him and He will give you the desires of your heart

Questions:

1. How does God's standard compare to your dating life?
2. What are the changes you need to make?
3. Are you trusting God?

Being Fruitful

Intro: What does it mean to be fruitful?

We Must Understand God's Promise (John 15:1-8)

1. What is the command?: To be fruitful...no to remain. Fruitfulness is not a command but a promise that is a result of our obedience. We are commanded to remain in Him. Unfruitfulness is a symptom of a deeper problem.

2. How do we remain? John 15:9-11: Obedience = Love. To remain is to practice radical obedience.

3. **What is the Fruit? (John 15:8, Galatians 5:22-28)** The fruit is Jesus. Jesus reproduces himself in us and through us. How? By using us to convert people and by continually changing us to be more like him.

We Must Understand Our Role (Luke 8:4-8, 11-15, Isaiah 55:8-11)

1. Our job is just to spread the seed (preach the word). We are not accountable for people's responses.
2. Our other job is to fight the weeds
3. God makes things grow. We just need to wholeheartedly obey and do our part; we cannot take credit or blame for the results. **(I Co 3:5-9)**

Questions:

1. What are some weeds that attack your faith?
2. What decisions do you need to makes in order to be victorious over them?

Two Becoming One

Read: I Peter 3:1-7

We need To Take Responsibility for Our Part

1. Our temptation is to think of our marriage or read this verse and focus on what our spouse needs to change, but we need to focus on our part. This verse challenges the wives to change their husbands not by what they say but by the example of their lives.
2. This principle applies to husbands & wives.
3. Our marriages will improve if we focus on the one thing that we control: Our own repentance. If we focus on being like Jesus rather than changing our spouse, it will give God an opportunity to work.

Read: Ephesians 5:22-33

Questions For Husbands:

1. What is your role in the marriage?
2. **(Read: Mark 10:41-45, John 13:1-17)** What does it mean to lead like Jesus? How are we to lead? Are you leading your spouse like Jesus?
3. What do you think it means to love your wife as Christ loved the church? What do you think you need to change in this area?

Homework: Ask your wife to read **Ephesians 5:22-33** and to suggest to you how you can change to be a better husband; then thank her and pray with her. Do not turn it around or get defensive. Take the correction and work to improve.

Questions For Wives:

1. What is your role in the marriage?
2. **(Read: I Peter 3:1-7)** What does it mean to submit to your husband? Does it mean being a doormat? Is submission one of your strengths? Why? Why not?
3. What do you think it means to respect your husband? What do you think you need to change in this area?

Homework: Ask your husband to read **Ephesians 5:22-33** and to suggest to you how you can change to be a better wife; then thank him and pray with him. Do not turn it around or get defensive. Take the correction and work to improve.

Old & New Testament

Is the Old Testament Still Important?

Yes!

1. It is still God's word **(Matthew 5: 17-20)**. Jesus fulfilled it but it still has great value.
2. **(Galatians 3:24)** It leads the way to Christ. We see God's plan unfold throughout history.
3. **(Romans 15:4)** Everything that happened and was recorded by the Holy Spirit was for our benefit, to teach us.
4. **(I Co 10:10-12)** It provides examples for us, positive and negative.
5. **(Hebrews 9:24-10:2)** Some of it is a shadow of the spiritual reality awaiting us, a physical representation of deep spiritual truths.

Is the Old Covenant Still Binding?

No!

1. **(Colossians 2:9-23)** The law (the Old Covenant) has been nailed to the cross.
2. All its regulations have been abolished (Sabbaths, holy days, sacrifices, etc.)
3. Jesus declared all food clean **(Mark 7:17-23, I Tim 4:1-5)**
4. **(Hebrews 8:6-13)** The New Covenant replaced the Old Covenant.

Questions:

    1. As Christians, do we still celebrate the Sabbath Day?
       Why? Why not?
    2. Is it wrong for Christians to eat certain foods, like pork,
       etc.
    3. Is it OK for Christians to ignore the Old Testament?
       Why? Why not?

The Main Thing

Intro: Heaven is our home and our goal. It needs to be one our main motivators. As Homework before this study, please read these scriptures: **(I Thessalonians 4: 13-18, I Co 9: 19-27, Philippians 3:7-16, II Co 5:1-10, II Peter 3: 3-13)**

The Main Thing Has Got to Be the Main Thing (I Co 15:19-20, 35-58)

1. Ultimately, heaven is all that matters. No matter what we accomplish, if we don't go to heaven our life is a failure. We've got to keep our eyes and our focus fixed on our eternal reward.
2. It will help us persevere through life's struggles. A heaven focus helps us keep our trials in perspective **(II Co 4:7-12, 16-18)**
3. A heaven focus helps us have the right priorities **(Luke 9:24-25)**
4. A heaven focus motivates us to share our faith **(II Co 5:11)**
5. Every decision we make in life is getting us closer to heaven or pulling us away.

Questions:

1. What kinds of decisions lead us closer to heaven?
2. What kind of decisions pull us away?
3. Is it obvious from the choices you make that heaven is your primary goal? Why? Why not?
4. What is something that you need to change to sharpen your heaven focus?
5. What do you look forward to the most about going to heaven?

"Three Things Before I Say Goodnight

Three Things Before I Say Goodnight:

I lock the door and dim the lights

I check the kids and tuck them in

If there's a noise, I check again.

But One day soon, my light will dim

And I will give account to Him

And I will have nothing to say

If unprepared I stand that day.

This night will come and I will stand

On Christ the rock or sinking sand

Did I obey when I was called?

Did I repent when I did fall?

Did I seek and serve and suffer

Bow down before no other?

The house, the car will burn like chaff.

Did they become my Golden Calf?

Or did I die my daily death

And preach until my dying breath?

Three Things Before I Say Goodnight

I pray the Lord will hold me tight

He'll tuck me in and dim the lights,

They'll be no blemish in his sight.

He'll kiss me as he lays me down

My soul will never touch the ground.

He'll wipe the tear drops from my eyes

Give me a crown, hand me a prize.

I pray that when my life is done

He'll turn to me and say, "Well done."

To follow Him while there is light,

To teach the lost and give them sight,

To Love the Lord with all my might,

Three Things Before I Say Goodnight

Daring To Dream

Intro: Jeremiah 29:11-13 God has plans for us, plans to prosper us, not to harm us. Homework before this study is to read **Genesis chapters 37, 39, 40, & 41.**

God Gave Him a Dream (Genesis 37: 1-11, 12-36, Genesis 41:46:)

1. **(Genesis 37:1-11)** God gave Joseph a dream. And in the dream God showed Joseph His vision for Joseph's life. Joseph was 17 when he saw this but 30 when it all came true (13 years of trials). God gave it to him and only him. No one else believed. Believing is our part. God will put dreams on your heart as well. Don't let anyone or anything discourage you.
2. **(Genesis 37:12-36)** Satan sets out to destroy our faith and crush our spirit. He can't destroy our dreams. They come from God. His goal is to get us to stop believing. Joseph's family, friends, and even his boss' wife put obstacle in Joseph's path, but by faith he persevered and saw God's vision for his life realized.

Questions

1. What are some dreams or goals that God has put on your heart?
2. What obstacles are in your way?
3. What lessons does Joseph provide for you? How can you be more like Joseph?
4. Should we be afraid to have great dreams for God?

Perseverance

Intro: Homework before this study – **Read: Genesis 39, 40, & 41.**

Questions:

1. How did Joseph display perseverance?
2. What motivated Joseph to be righteous in every circumstance? What circumstances tempt you to be unrighteous?
3. Have you ever lost patience with God? How and why?
4. What are some keys to persevering?

Read (Romans 5:1-5, I Co 10:12-13, James 1:2-4, II Co 1:3-11)

Questions:

1. Does God allow us to be tested more than we can bear? How does that make you feel?
2. What positive things come from our suffering? How does it build our character? How does it make us more like Jesus?
3. What are some ways the faith of others benefits from our struggles?
4. Why should we never despair or lose hope?

Forgiveness

Intro: Let's talk about forgiveness

Read: Genesis 5:15-21

Questions:

1. What kind of suffering had Joseph brothers put him through?
2. From a human point of view, did Joseph have the right to be angry and seek revenge?
3. What can we learn about our need to forgive from Joseph's example?

Read: (Matthew 18: 21-35, Mt 6:14-15, Romans 12:14-21)

Questions:

1. What is God's attitude toward us when we are unforgiving? Why?
2. Do we ever have the right to withhold our forgiveness from somebody? Why? Why not?
3. How are we to treat those who mistreat us? What if they refuse to stop?
4. What is the hardest thing about this for you?
5. Who have you not forgiven?   What is holding you back?

Radical Purity

Intro: For Homework before this study, read **Genesis Chapter 39.**

Read Genesis 39:1-18

1. What lessons can we learn about avoiding sexual sin from Joseph?
2. Why did he run out?   What are some situations we need to run from?
3. What was Joseph's motivation? Who would have known if Joseph sinned in secret?

Read: (Job 31:1, Mt 5:27-30, Mark 7:20-23, Ephesians 5:1-3)

Questions:
1. What does it mean to be impure when it comes to sexual sin? Give some examples?
2. Is lust a sin? How would you define it?
3. What about pornography? Self-gratification? Does God consider it sin? Why? Why not?
4. If you're unmarried, are all kinds of sexual activity sin? What about making out? How do you think these things make God feel?
5. According to **Mt 5:27-30**, how radical should we be about dealing with sin? What are some practical ways to apply this passage to sexual sin?
6. How can **Ecclesiastes 4:9-12** help us in overcoming sexual sin. What are some ways other disciples can help us stay pure.
7. How important is **James 5:16** in helping us overcome sexual sin?

Stewardship Part I
(Finding Your Gift)

1 Peter 4:10
10Each one should use whatever gift he has received to serve others, faithfully administering God's grace in its various forms.

From the beginning, God intended that we be good stewards or managers of everything He created and instituted. This includes our spiritual gifts as well as material blessings.
These next three sections will address God's desire for us to freely give as we've been given to.
God, through 1st Peter 4:10, teaches us that everyone has been blessed with gifts from Him. Some are more aware of this than others. Here are a few ways to identify your gifts.

    1.) Pray and ask God **(Daniel 2:21-23)**
        a.) God alone knows what we do best. Pray for Him to expose and reveal your talents and Gifts.

    2.) Take note of your uniqueness and experiences **(Acts 7:20-22)**
        a.) Recognize that God has placed extraordinary talents in each and every one of us, even before we decided to follow Him.
        b.) He has also placed us in situations that have sharpened those talents and helped us to develop new skills.
        c.) Remember, like Moses, how and where we were raised. Our education and job experience are all things that have shaped our gifts for the purpose of glorifying God.

3.) Ask good friends **(Proverbs 20:5, 2nd Peter 3:15-16)**

    a.) Ask people who know you what they see as your strengths.

    b.) Peter spoke about Paul in his writings as having the wisdom that God gave him.

    c.) Peter identified Paul's gifts, understood his strengths and was able to communicate what they were.

Questions:

    1.) Have you taken time to pray about your talent and gifts and using them for God?

    2.) Have you taken time to meditate on the special unique skills God has given you?

    3.) What were some of the things you excelled in before becoming a Christian?

    4.) How can they be used in God's Kingdom?

Encouragement:

- Take some time during this study to ask a friend what they see as your strengths. Pray together about how they can be used for God's glory.
- Write them down and ask God to magnify them often.

Stewardship Part II
(Serving)

A young boy was walking along a beach and happened upon a genie in a bottle. It was the genie's custom to grant the owner of the bottle a wish but he encouraged the boy to choose wisely. The boy meditated and finally told the genie he wished to know the difference between heaven and hell. The genie thought the young man had chosen a fine wish and proceeded to show him the difference between heaven and hell. He first showed him hell. There the boy saw a multitude of people encircled around a smorgasbord of food. Each person held in his hand a six-foot spoon, which was used to bring food from the middle of the circle. He also noticed the multitude was starving because they could not maneuver the weight of the food and the spoon back to their mouths. The genie then took him to heaven, where strangely the boy saw the same scenario, a multitude of people encircled around a smorgasbord of food but here the people seemed happy and joyful. The genie asked the boy if he knew the difference between heaven and hell. The boy answered yes. In hell people suffered because they tried to feed themselves but in heaven they were happy and well nourished. They were unable to feed themselves but they were able to feed each other.

Life in the church is much like this story. It illustrates how the church functions best and flourishes when every member is striving to serve. Our spiritual growth and growth as a body are directly proportional to using our gifts and considering others better than ourselves.

1.) We were saved to serve **(Phil 2: 3-8)**
        a.) Our motivation for serving should be
          Christ who was the ultimate servant.

2.) We will be held accountable for how we use our gifts.
(Mt 25:14-29, Luke 16: 1-2, 1st Co 4: 1-2)
        a.) God will expect us to account for the
          use of our gifts.

3.) We serve one another **(1st Peter 4:10)**

Questions:
   1.) Where and how do you see yourself serving in the
   church, in the community?
   2.) Ask a friend how they see you serving.
   3.) Write down some areas you'd like to grow to serve in.
Encouragement:
   • Put these goals of serving to daily prayer.
   • Ask others to pray about it as well.

Stewardship Part III
(Finances)

God desires that we be good stewards of all the blessings He
has bestowed upon us. This includes, but is not exclusive to, our
time, efforts and talents. We are also called to be good stewards
of our material and monetary blessings. This particular section
will focus on financial giving but it is important to remember
that this is only one aspect of being good financial stewards. We
are also called to manage our debt **(Rom 13:8)**, to watch out for
the temptations of wealth **(1Tim 6:9)** and instructed on how to
guard our hearts and maintain proper perspective if we are rich
(1 Tim 6:17-17). As a reminder, many of these passages are not
exclusive to financial sacrifice.

Deuteronomy 16
*17 Each of you must bring a gift in proportion to the way the
LORD your God has blessed you.*

2nd Corinthians 8 and 9
The reason for the collection in 2nd Corinthians 8 and 9 seemed
to be for serving poor Christians in Jerusalem, there is no doubt
that the principals for giving are the same even when the need is
different.

Why Give
    1.) His Love
            a.) We our motivated by a sincere love and
                gratitude for what God has done for us **(1st
                John 4:19)**.
            b.) We give because we've given first to the
                Lord **(2nd Co 8:5)**.
            c.) We cannot earn or repay the gift but we
                remember daily we are **Saved to Serve (2nd
                Co 9:12)**.

2.) Our Salvation
    a.) Being saved puts us in a unique place to give back to God **(2nd Co 9:13)**.
    b.) God's children are the pledged supporters of His work **(2nd Co 9:13)**.
    c.) We have been given much, Christ, the cross and forgiveness. We are called to freely give **(Luke 12:47-49)**.

3.) Their Need
    d.) There are billions of people in the world needing to here the gospel message. This will not happen without the sacrifice of time, lives and money **(2 Pet 3:8-9, Mt 28:18-20, 2nd Co 9:12)**.
    e.) This encourages equality in giving. Instead of the old adage of 20% of the people doing 80% of the work, all can equally share in helping to meet whatever need will arise **(2nd Co 8:13-15)**.

How We Should Give
1.) Give With a pure Heart
    a.) We should give not out of competitiveness, or to be recognized but with a pure heart and motive **(Mt 6:1-4)**.
    b.) We should give from a joyful, cheerful heart. We should desire to give not motivated by reluctance, unbiblical pressure, duress or compulsion **(Luke 12:24, 2nd Co 9:7-8)**.

2.) Give Generously
    a.) We are instructed to give generously, as God has blessed us. **(Pro11:25-28, Mt 6:21, 2nd Co 8:1-5, 2nd Co 9:6)**

        b.) We need to see generosity and giving as a gift of God to be used for His glory **(Rom 12:8).**

3.) Give Sacrificially

        a.) The question may arise, how much should I give? What is an acceptable sacrifice to God? What about tithing?

        b.) Ultimately what you've decided to give should be between you and God but based on biblical principals **(2nd Co 9:7).**

        c.) The impoverished church of Macedonia was commended for their sacrificial giving, as was the widow who put in two copper coins **(2nd Co 8:1-4, Mark 12:41-43).**

4.) Excel in the Grace of Giving

        a.) Jesus instructed His followers that their righteousness must exceed that of the Pharisees and teachers of the law who were content with doing the bare minimum. This included tithing. **(Mt 5:20, Mt 23:23).**

        b.) Though tithing can be a great starting place for the new convert it should not be our end goal. God should get our first fruits and best effort **(Mal 1:6-9).** We should give as God has blessed us **(Pro 11:24).** Give in keeping with our income (1st Co 16:2) and give out of sacrifice and not wealth **(Mark 12:21-23).**

        c.) Lastly we need to excel in the grace of giving. This means to grow in our ability to give, a free gift to God, without wanting anything in return **(2nd Co 8:7).**

A Helpful Quote:

"It is then not a question of how much of our substance we are willing to give to the Lord but, on the contrary, the problem is, "How much of what the Lord has entrusted to me shall I keep?"
James Burton Coffman

Questions:
1.) Am I giving to the Lord first?
2.) How are my motives and heart on giving?
3.) Is my giving a first fruit offering and is it sacrificial?
4.) Have you decided what to give? Is it consistent and in keeping with your income?

The Lord's Supper

Intro: (Communion)

Within the body of Christ there are some amazing but rare opportunities to function and focus on the worship of God in total congregational harmony. Prayer and song certainly are two that come to mind but it is The Lord's Supper or Communion that is exclusive and unique to the Christian community.

Why The Communion:
Jesus himself instituted a practice of remembrance. Prior to his death, Jesus gave instructions to the twelve that when they came together, they were to take time to remember His sacrifice **(Luke 22:19-20, 1st Co 11:23-26).**

a.) Remembrance of His life, the way He lived but especially the way He died: This is not so much a focus on the brutality of His death but His submission to God **(Mt 26:39).**

b.) Remembrance of a new covenant offered only through the blood of Christ: This is a covenant of forgiveness that we entered into when we became new creations **(Luke 22:20, Mt 26:28).**

c.) **(1st Co 11:26)** For whenever you eat this bread and drink this cup, you proclaim the Lord's death until he comes. Through our unified observance of The Lord's Supper we participate in congregational pronouncement of our amazing savior (Pretty cool).

How Should We Receive the Communion?

Looking Inward

a.) Participating in the Lord's Supper requires that we must examine ourselves to insure that our focus is Christ and His sacrifice. It is a remembrance and a celebration. Anything less than this is to receive the communion in an unworthy manner. **(1st Co 11:27-29)**

Looking Backward

b.) The communion helps us look back to the cross. It is a constant reminder that Christians not only participate in the life of Christ but His death and resurrection as well. **(Rom 6:3, Phil 3:10)**

Looking Forward

c.) The time is coming when Jesus will celebrate the communion on His return. We look back to remember the cross but we also look forward to a new beginning and to be called home. **(Mt 26:27-29, 1st Co 11:26)**

Questions:

1.) What does it mean to receive the Lord's Supper in an unworthy manner? Are any of us ever worthy or deserving?

2.) What types of things should you focus on during the communion?

3.) Why is self-examination important?

For more reading on this subject:
In Remembrance of Me
Enriching Our Understanding of the Lord's Supper
by Andrew C. Fleming

Your First Love

Intro: What does it mean to love God?

Lordship = Love (Luke 10:27, John 14:14-21, I John 5:2-3)

Questions:

1. What does it mean to love God with all of your mind?
2. What about all your heart? All your strength? All your soul?
3. Why is this so important to God?
4. What is the behavior of someone who loves God this way? Would it be obvious? Why? Why not?
5. Is it possible to love God this way and not be obedient to His word?   Should obedience be a burden?

Love Means Making Every Effort (Luke 13:22-25, Matthew 7:13-14)

1. They ask Jesus if only a few are going to be saved. What is the answer?
2. What is the key to making it?
3. Is there a difference between trying and making every effort? Explain.
4. How can we tell if we are giving God our best?
5. When it comes to loving God, are you trying or making every effort?

Remember the Call

Intro: Sometimes it's important to have reminders.

Remember Your First Love (Revelation 2: 1-7)

Questions:

1. What are some positives Jesus shares about this church?
2. What were the negatives?
3. What does it mean to lose your first love?
4. What kind of things can steal our love?
5. What are the signs?

Keys to Staying in Love (II Peter 1:3-11)

Questions:

1. How can we make our calling and election sure?
2. What are some ways we can add these qualities in increasing measure? What allows these qualities to grow?
3. What types of things stunt our growth?
4. **(Matthew 4:4, Romans 10:17)** What roles do Bible study and prayer have? How important is it to be consistent?
5. Is daily, quality Bible study and prayer a reality for you?

Radical Faith

Intro: For homework, before doing this study, read (**Hebrews chapter 11, Genesis chapter 18, and Genesis 21:1-7**).

Overcome Facts With Faith (Romans 4:18-22, Genesis 18:9-15)

Questions:

1. What was God's promise to Abraham?
2. What were the obstacles in his way?
3. Why did Sarah laugh? What are some ways we laugh at God?
4. Does having faith mean ignoring the facts, having blind faith? Why? Why not?
5. How was Abraham able to face the facts and still not waver?
6. What are some signs that we are wavering in our faith?
7. What types of things make your faith waver?
8. **(Hebrews 11:5-6)** How important is faith to God? Why is it so important?
9. How can you be more like Abraham and the heroes of faith in Hebrews 11

Practical Grace

Intro: (II Timothy 2:1) We need to be strong in the grace.

Grace Changes Everything (I Peter 2:9-12, I Timothy 1:12-17)

Outside of God's Grace:

1. We don't belong to God
2. We do not receive God's mercy. **(Isaiah 59:1-2)** We are still in our sins.
3. We are not His people.
4. We are in the dark, spiritually.

Inside God's Grace:

1. We are God's chosen people.
2. We are God's priests.
3. **(Psalm 103:8-13)** We always see God's mercy. All of our sins are forgiven. They never happened.
4. We are in the light, spiritually.

Questions:

1. As a Christian, through Jesus' blood **(Mt 26:27-28),** we live in God's grace. How does that make you feel?
2. **(I Co 15:1-11)** How did receiving God's grace effect Paul? How should it motivate us?

Quiz: How do we know we don't understand grace?

1. We feel guilty all the time
2. We rarely feel convicted about sin? **(Romans 6: 1-4, Hebrews 10:29)**
3. We need an outside force to motivate us
4. We hold Grudges **(Hebrews 12:15)**
5. We feel Like God has forgotten us.
6. Obedience is a burden
7. We take sin lightly.
8. We're ungrateful
9. We never feel like we're good enough.
10. Whenever we go through trials we believe God is punishing us.

Quiz: How do we know we understand grace?

1. We're thankful
2. We're quick to Forgive **(Matthew 6:14-15)**
3. We're hardworking **(I Co 15: 9-10)**
4. Practice radical repentance **(Titus 2 :11)**
5. Obedience is a joy and a privilege **(I John 5:3)**
6. We are quick to serve
7. We're slow to judge
8. Our motivation comes from inside out. **(I Thess. 1:2-3)**
9. We're confident of our salvation **(Romans 8: 31-39)**
10. We're soft hearted

Race & Racism

Intro: As Christians, how should we deal with racism? For homework before doing this study, read **(Galatians 3:26-28, Colossians 3:11, Galatians 2:11-21. II Co 5:14-21, James 2:1-12)**

Questions:

1. Have you ever experienced prejudice or racism? How? How did it make you feel?
2. **(Galatians 3:26-28, Colossians 3:11)** How does God's view of race and class differ from the world's?
3. Is God bothered by interracial couples? Does he show favoritism to the wealthy? Does he only spend time with certain kinds of people?
3. What are some ways we can see people from a worldly point of view? **(II Co 5:16-21)** Do you sometimes pre-judge people based on race? Income? Age? Appearance? How does that make God feel?
4. Why did Paul confront Peter in **(Galatians 2:11-21)**? How should we approach it when we see prejudice in the church?
5. Is it OK in God's sight for us to pick our congregation based on the race or culture of its members? What about the race of its leaders? How does that make God feel?
6. **(John 17:20-23)** What was Jesus' prayer for the church? What are some ways we can help fulfill his dream?

Church Discipline

What Does It Mean To Fall Away?

D. **(Mt 11:6, 26:31, 26:33, Mark 4:17, Luke 8:13, II Peter
    1:10, Mt 18:12-13, I Timothy 1:6, 6:10, 6:20-21, II
    Tim. 2:17-18, II Peter 2:15 James 5:19, I Timothy
    1:19, I Tim 4:1)** It is called wandering from the faith,
    falling away, shipwrecking our faith, etc. When we
    refuse to repent of sin or cut ourselves off from Christ's
    body we turn our back on Christ.

E. **(Hebrews 10:26-31)** Once in this state, we are outside of
    God's grace.

F. **(Galatians 6:1-2, James 5:20)** If someone repents, he
    can be restored back to fellowship with Christ

G. **(Hebrews 6: 4-6)** If we allow our hearts to be hardened,
    we can reach a point of no return.

What Does It Mean To Be In Fellowship?

A. **(I Co 5:1-5, 9-12)** Fellowship with Christ's body may be
    removed because of sin. In fact, the Bible commands that
    the congregation's leadership invoke church discipline in
    certain situations. The goal is to discipline the brother or
    sister who is in sin in hopes of inspiring repentance.

1. Immorality and rebellious sin **(I Co 5:1-5, 9-12)**

2. Divisiveness **Titus 3:9-11**

3. Idleness **(II Thessalonians 3:6-10)** (Greek: Atakos/
    undisciplined, disorderly, out of rank, disorderly in an
    undisciplined or insubordinate manner; idly, lazily,
    indolently. **[Taken fro the Key Word Study Bible]**

B. **(II Co 2:5-11)** The individual is restored to fellowship with the body when he has adequately displayed repentance

Questions:

1. What are the signs that someone has wandered from the faith?
2. Is it possible to purposely abandon fellowship from Christ's body and be in fellowship with Christ? Why? Why not?
3. Why is it important to impose church discipline? What is the goal?
4. Why is it important to be careful when restoring someone who is in sin?

Carrying the Mat

Intro: (Ecclesiastes 4:9-12) We need strong spiritual friendships. As homework, before this study, please read the excerpt from Closer Than a Brother at the end and study the scriptures listed there.

We Need to Help Each Other See Jesus (Luke 5:17-20)

Questions:
1. What stands out to you about this man's friends?
2. Was Jesus impressed by his friends?
3. Why is it important to have spiritual friendships?
4. What are some practical ways that we can carry the mat for each other?
5. Is Jesus impressed by the faith of your friends? **(II Co 15:33-34)** How does bad company effect good character?

We Need to Sharpen One Another (Proverbs 27:17, 18:24, 17:17, Hebrews 3:13, Hebrews 10:23-25)
Question:

1. What type of friendships are these passages describing?
2. What is the goal of these relationships?
3. What are some ways that we can build these types of friendships?
4. What does it mean for iron to sharpen iron? How can we achieve this?
5. How important is it that we encourage each other, daily?
6. What are some practical ways that we can encourage each other?

7. Do you have these types of spiritual friendships? If not, how do you plan to build some?

(Below is an excerpt from <u>Closer Than a Brother</u>, pages 55-62, that should be helpful)

Love is the Method I Co 13:1-8 John 13:34-35 Is the ultimate one another scripture, stating, *"A new command I give you: Love one another. As I have loved you, so you must love one another. By this all men will know that you are my disciples, if you love one another."*

We could spend a lifetime gleaming lessons from this one scripture; yet, there are a few fundamental lessons that leap out at us. First, loving one another in this way is a mark of discipleship, a large part of what sets Jesus' disciples apart from the rest of the world. Displaying this supernatural love is what makes us stand out, shining like a light on a hill. This love is truly supernatural, so only through depending on the Spirit do we have hope of obeying this command. Jesus instructs His church to love each other the way that He loves us. This means that our love for each other must be unconditional. It is not based on what someone has done for us or whether he/she reciprocates. We do not serve only our friends or disciples that we know personally. We extend this love to all of our brothers and sisters, free of charge with no strings attached. Jesus' love is color blind, culture blind, appearance blind, and class blind.

Jesus loves without limit, laying down His life for us. Likewise,
he calls us to lay down our lives for our brothers and sisters
(I John 3:16). Jesus loves intimately. He does not love from a
distance. We need to build intimate relationships in the body of
Christ. I believe that all the one another passages in the Bible,
the ones that use the phrase one another and the ones that
describe this concept with different terminology, are designed to
help us to understand how to love each other the way Jesus
loves us. He breaks it down piece-by-piece, scripture by
scripture, not leaving it up to our own imaginations. When we
truly put these passages into practice, personally and in our
churches, it will unleash the power of Christ's love like never
before.

Below is a sampling of some of the one another commands from
the scriptures:

**(*Please, take a few minutes to study these
scriptures. Everything written in the next few
chapters is based on the commands and principles
from these passages.)**

*A. Colossians 3: 16: "Let the word of Christ dwell in you
richly as you teach and admonish one another with all wisdom, and
as you sing psalms, hymns and spiritual songs with gratitude in*

your hearts to God." This passage commands us to admonish one another. This is a word that doesn't get used very often in every day speech. Although preachers use the word admonish in their sermons from time to time, most members (and many preachers) have no idea about the true meaning of the word so we don't truly understand the nature of this command. The word translated admonish in this passage comes from the Greek word Noutheteo: Meaning to Teach and Admonish (to rebuke mildly, advise strongly-to warn someone of their error, alert them to the consequences of their error, and to show them the means of correcting their problem) This is a weighty command, a command that can only truly be obeyed among individuals committed to having intimate spiritual friendships. **{Definition taken The Hebrew-Greek Key Word Study Bible page 1654}**

B. James 5: 16: *"Therefore confess your sins to each other and pray for each other so that you may be healed. The prayer of a righteous man is powerful and effective."* This verse commands us to confess our sins to one another and to pray for each other. Confessing our sins to each other so we can help and pray for each other is a command from

God not a request. Just confessing our sins to God is not enough. He desires that we confess to one another.

C. Galatians 5: 13: *"You, my brothers, were called to be free. But do not use your freedom to indulge the sinful nature; rather, serve one another in love"* We are commanded us to serve one another. The Greek word translated serve here is Douleuo (which means to be a slave, stand as a slave to another). God has bound us to each other, compelling us by Christ's love to serve each other. **{Definition taken The Hebrew-Greek Key Word Study Bible page 1611}**

D. I Thessalonians 5: 11: *"Therefore encourage one another and build each other up, just as in fact you are doing."* We are commanded to encourage one another.

E. Heb 3:13: *"But encourage one another daily, as long as it is called Today, so that none of you may be hardened by sin's deceitfulness."* This passage takes it a step further commanding us to encourage one another daily. There is nothing that we need more from our brothers and sisters than encouragement.

F. Hebrews 10: 24: *"And let us consider how we may spur one another on toward love and good deeds."* We are told to consider how we can spur one another on toward love and good deeds.   This is more than just the responsibility of the evangelists and elders.   We all have a responsibility to spur on our brothers and sisters.

G. Colossians 3: 13: *"Bear with each other and forgive whatever grievances you may have against one another. Forgive as the Lord forgave you"* We are commanded to forgive one another. We all need grace because messing up is what we do best. We need to extend grace to each other.

H. Ephesians 4: 2: *"Be completely humble and gentle; be patient, bearing with one another in love."* This scripture commands us to be patient with one another. This passage   is   tailor   made   for   husbands   and wives…roommates too.

I. Ephesians 4: 32: *"Be kind and compassionate to one another, forgiving each other, just as in Christ God forgave you."* We are commanded to have compassion for one another. We need empathy for others' circumstances, and to understand that meeting needs in the church is not just the responsibility of leadership or a specific ministry. It is all of our responsibility.

J. Ephesians 5: 21: *"Submit to one another out of reverence for Christ."* Commands us to submit to one other. Humility has great healing power.

K. Romans 12:16 *Live in harmony with one another. Do not be proud, but be willing to associate with people of low position. Do not be conceited."* Commands us to live in harmony with one another.

L. Romans 12:10: *"Be devoted to one another in brotherly love. Honor one another above yourselves."* Commands us to honor one another above ourselves. Too often, I am my own favorite person. This is a powerful, challenging scripture.

M. Romans 12:10: *"Be devoted to one another in brotherly love. Honor one another above yourselves."* Commands us to be devoted to one another. Without devotion it is impossible to build family.

N. Romans 15:7: *"Accept one another, then, just as Christ accepted you, in order to bring praise to God."* Commands us to accept one another as Christ accepted us. We are all fruits and nuts with our own quirks and foibles and lots of baggage. In addition, we come from different generations, different races, different economic groups, different cultures, and even different corners of the earth. There is great power in this passage.

O. Proverbs 27:17: *"As iron sharpens iron, so one man sharpens another."*

P. Proverbs 18:24: *"A man of many companions may come to ruin, but there is a friend who sticks closer than a brother."*

Q. Proverbs 17:17: *" A friend loves at all times, and a brother is born for adversity."*

R. Proverbs 15:22: *"Plans fail for lack of counsel, but with many advisers they succeed."*

S. Ephesians 4: 15-16: *"Instead, speaking the truth in love, we will in all things grow up into him who is the Head, that is, Christ. From him the whole body, joined and held together by every supporting ligament, grows and builds itself up in love, as each part does its work."* This passage encourages us to speak the truth in love to one another. Too often the truth is rare and truth speakers are an endangered species.

T. *I Peter 4:8**: *"Love each other deeply, because love covers over a multitude of sins."* **I Peter 1:22** is a sister passage.

These passages present a road map, designed to take us to an amazing destination while traveling down a narrow road. Come; let us continue our journey, following in the footsteps of Jesus every step of the way. I am sure He will make it worth our while.

Small Groups

Intro: Our goal is to be a church modeled after (**Acts 2:42-47**). That's the goal. How do we get there from here? One of the keys is small group fellowship. What are the biblical principles?

The Jethro Principle (Exodus 18:9-27)

> This is God's inspired word
> Everything that was written in the past was written
>   to teach us. **(Romans 15:4, I Co 10:11)**.
> Moses was instructed to break down the nation Israel
>   into groups of tens, hundreds, and thousands in
>   order to meet needs.

The Jesus Principle (Luke 6:12, Mark 3:13-14, 3 Luke 9: 28-36 Luke 10: 1, Mark 10: 41-45)

A. **(Mark 10: 41-45)** Jesus defined biblical leadership as servant leadership.
B. Jesus, the most capable leader in all creation, did not try to do it alone. He spent most of His time not with the crowds but with smaller groups (the 72, the 12, and the 3), and spent the greatest amount time with the 3 and the 12.
C. **(Mt 28. 18-20, Luke 24:45-49, Acts 1:6-8)** He sent the remaining 11 out to carry on his work.

The Church (II Timothy 2:1-2, Ephesians 4:11-16)

A. **(II Timothy 2:1-2)** Timothy was told to entrust his teaching to reliable men who in turn can pass on what they had learned to others?
B. **(Ephesians 4:11-16)** Leadership is put in place by God to prepare God's people for works of service.

Questions:

> 1. Do you think there are similarities between the Jethro principle and Jesus' ministry? How? How not?
> 2. Why do you think Jesus focused on a few? What can we learn from that example?
> 3. Do you think it is likely that Timothy imitated Jesus' method as he trained his reliable men? Why? Why not?
> 4. What are some ways small groups can be used to prepare God's church for works of service? How can they help foster family? Meet needs?

The Mission

Intro: For homework before this study, read **(Ezekiel 33:1-9, Acts 3:8-22, John 4:1-42)**

We Have Been Called to Evangelize the World

1. **(Matthew 28:19-20)** This is the last thing Jesus commanded. **(Luke 24:47, Mark 16:15, Acts 1:6- 8)**.
2. It was the first thing Jesus commanded from His disciples **(Mark 1:6-18)**
3. It is the second part of the greatest commandment. **Matthew 22: 37-(39) (Love your neighbor as yourself)**.
4. **Jesus wept over the lost (Luke 19:41-44)**
5. His last words on the cross expressed concern of the souls of His enemies **(Luke 23:34)**.
6. It was Jesus' stated purpose **(Luke 19:10, Mark 1:35-39)**

Questions:

1. How important is it to Jesus that we carry on His mission?
2. Why is it so important?
3. What was Jesus' motivation? What should ours be?
4. Are you devoted to the mission? How's it going?

We Should Make the Most of Every Opportunity
(Ephesians 5:15, John 4:1-42)

Questions:

1. What do you think it means to make the most of every opportunity?
2. How is John 4 an example of this?
3. What are some opportunities that you need to better utilize?

The Tongue

Intro: The tongue is powerful.

Read: (James 3:1-12, Proverb 12:18, Proverbs 15:1, Proverbs 21:23, Proverbs 25:15)

The Tongue Can Tear Us Apart (Proverbs 10: 31-32, 11:9, 12, 13, 18:6-8, Ephesians 4: 20-29, Colossians 3:8-9)

Questions:

1. What are some ways that the tongue can be hurtful?
2. What is God's view toward gossip?
3. What are some ways we can avoid gossip?
4. What is your biggest challenge when it comes to the tongue?

The Tongue Can Change the World   (Proverbs 18:21, Proverbs 24:11-12, Hebrews 3:13)

Questions:

1. How does the tongue have power over life and death?
2. How can we use it for life?

Spiritual Authority

Intro. For homework, before this study, read: **(John 13:1-17, John 10:1-18, Numbers 12:1-16).**

God Establishes All Authority

1. **(Ephesians 6:1-3, Colossians 3:20)** We need to obey our parents.
2. **(Romans 13:1-7, Mt 22:21)** Christians need to obey civil authorities.
3. Spiritual authority has been put in place by God **(Ephesians 4: 11, I Tim 5:17-20, Titus 1:5-9, 2:1-8).**
4. Spiritual authority must not be abused **(Mark 10:41-45, John 13:1-17, John 10:1-18).** Jesus is the example.
5. Spiritual Authority should be respected **(Hebrews 13: 7, 17, Numbers 12:1-16).**
6. In the church, delegated authority is often necessary **(II Tim 2:2, Acts 6:1-6)**

Questions:

1. How does spiritual leadership differ from worldly leadership?
2. Why is it important for disciples to obey civil authority?
3. In the church, how can we make the job of our leaders a burden? How can we make it a joy?

Rejoice

Be Joyful Always **(Philippians 4:4-7, 8-9, Philippians 3:12-16, Philippians 4:10-13)**

Questions:

1. (Phil 4:4-7) What makes this command so challenging?
2. From these scriptures, what are some keys to being joyful?
3. What can we learn from **(Phil 3:12-16)?**
4. What is the secret to being content in every situation?

Do Not Worry (Mt 6: 25-33)

Questions:
1. Why do we worry?
2. About what do you worry?
3. What does God say about worrying? Is God saying not to be responsible?
4. What are some things that can help you not to worry?

Shining Like Stars

Intro: What does it mean to be successful? Is it wrong to be ambitious?

We Need to Shine for the World

(Philippians 2: 14-16, Romans 2: 3:5-11)

    A. What kind of ambition is God talking about in these passages? How is it different from the world?

    B. Is it wrong to seek glory, honor, and immortality? Why? Why not?

    C. What are some ways we can shine like stars for God?

We Need to Shine for Eternity (Daniel 12:1-4, Proverbs 11:30)

    A. From these passages, what is the key to shining like stars?

    B. How does God feel about saving souls? To Him, is there anything more important?

    C. What do you want your legacy to be?

Spiritual Warfare

We Are in A Spiritual War (Ephesians 6:10-20, II Co 10:1-6)

Questions:

1. We are in a spiritual war. What is at stake? How are we under attack?
2. What is Satan's primary weapon against you?
3. What are some of the weapons at our disposable?
4. How can we utilize them practically?
5. **(Romans 12:9-21)** Is love a weapon? How?

The Day of Evil Will Come (Luke 6: 46-49)

Questions:
1. What are some ways we can be attacked by spiritual flood waters?
2. What is the key to surviving the flood?
3. What does it mean to build our lives on the rock? How can we do it practically?
4. If we trust our feelings and opinions more than the word, is that a good foundation? Why? Why not?
5. How important is daily Bible study and prayer to all this? How is that going for you?

Recommended Fiction that Illustrates Spiritual Warfare:

1. The Screw Tape Letters by C.S. Lewis
2. Shadow Dancers by F. Barton Davis
3. This Present Darkness by Frank Peretti

Don't Look Back

Intro: Romans 15:4

Don't Look Back (Gen 18:16-33, Genesis 19:15-29)

Questions:

1. How do you see God's judgment from this account?
2. How do you see God's grace?
3. Why do you think Lot's wife looked back? If you were her, would you have been tempted to look back?
4. **(Luke 9:57-62)** Can focusing too much on the past negatively affect our spiritual lives? How?
5. Is it sometimes tempting to lose faith or pull back because of past hurts? Past sins? What does God want us to do in those situations?

Don't Stop (Gen 19:24-26)

Questions:

1. Where was Lot commanded to go?
2. What did God have planned for Lot in the mountains? Do you think God had a plan? Why? Why not?
3. What did Lot do instead? Why?
4. Have you ever let fear stop you from obeying God? How?
5. What should we do when we are tempted to give in to fear?
6. What would be different in you life if you totally lived by faith, not fear?

Times of Testing

Intro: (Hebrews 4:14-16, Hebrews 5:7-10)

Questions:

1. How would you define temptation?
2. Can something be tempting with out being desirable to you on some level?
3. What are your chief temptations?
4. We are told in Hebrews that Jesus was tempted in every way just as we are but never sinned. Since this is true, what kind of temptations did Jesus have?
5. What was the role of prayer in His resisting sin?

Read: (Mt 4:1-11, Luke 4:1-13)

Questions:

1. Why do you think Satan chose the temptations he chose?
2. What were some of the temptations used? Why were they tempting?
3. How did Jesus resist? What can we learn from His answers?
4. What was the importance of using scripture to refute each attempt? How can we imitate this?
5. What does (**Mt 4:4**) mean? How is the word our food? How often do we need to eat? What are the consequences if we do not?
6. (**Luke 4:13**) What does it mean that he left for a more opportune time? What are the situations for you that Satan feels are opportune?
7. (**Romans 10:14-17**) How can we build up our faith?

Integrity

Intro: **How would you define integrity?**

Integrity Has Value (Proverbs 16:8, Psalm 73)

1. **(Pro 16:8)** We know that this passage is true (It's God's word), but does it always feel true? Is it practical? Why? Why not?
2. What is the biggest challenge in living this way?
3. Have you ever felt like the author of **Psalm 73** did in the first part of that Psalm? What made you feel that way?
4. How should you feel?

Deceit Has a Price (Proverbs 11:3, Acts 4:32-37, Act 5:1-11, Rev 21:8, Colossians 3:9)

Questions:

1. Why was Ananias struck dead? What was his crime? Was the issue money or honesty?
2. What value does God put on honesty? Why is it so important to God?
3. From a worldly point of view, wasn't Ananias' lie a little lie? How do you think God feels when we lie?
4. Is there such a thing as a little lie? Is there ever a good reason to lie? Why? Why not?
5. (Proverbs 11:3) What are some ways that deceit can destroy our lives?
6. When are you most tempted to lie?
7. Have you totally repented of deceit?

Spiritual Revival

Intro: What should we do when we need spiritual revival?

Exhale (Mark 7:14-23, Galatians 5:19-21, Colossians 3: 1-11)

Questions:

1. What type of things do we need to get out of our systems?
2. Which of these is a struggle for you? How so?
3. What are some keys to getting it out?
4. What are some decisions you need to make in order to make a change?
5. **(Galatians 6:1-5)** How can we carry each other's burdens?
6. Who are you allowing to help you? Who are you helping?

Inhale (Colossians 3:1-4, 12-17, Galatians 5:22-26)

Questions:

1. What does it mean to set our minds on things above?
2. How can we do it practically?
3. What are some keys to growing in putting these qualities to our lives?
4. **(Luke 11:24-26, James 4:13-17)** Is it effective to attempt to turn from sin without replacing the sin with something Godly? Why? Why not?
5. Why is it important to do the good we know we ought to do? Give me some examples
6. What decisions are you ready to make?

Excellence

Mark 7:37
People were overwhelmed with amazement. "He has done everything well," they said. "He even makes the deaf hear and the mute speak.

The goal of every follower of Christ is our best effort. That effort is not made only when we are involved in spiritual matters but all matters of life. With Jesus everything was a spiritual issue, we see how He pleased God in all He did. This should be our goal as well. We can't be the best at all things but we certainly can do our best at all things.
Here are a few areas that sometimes require special attention to be excellent.

Excellence in Spiritual Growth (2nd Peter 1:5-9)
a.) The bible encourages us to make every effort to grow spiritually. We are to add to our foundational knowledge of faith and build towards maturity.
b.) The initial planting and watering we received at conversion shouldn't cease. We still need constant gardening, watering and the turning over of soil to become what God desires.
c.) Making the effort to grow prevents us from being ineffective and unproductive.

Excellence on the Job (Col 3:22-24)
a.) Here in Colossians the bible instructs us to do all things as though we are working for the Lord.
b.) We are to have the same work ethic whether the eyes of our employers, teachers, coaches, parents or spouse are on us or not. No matter what we do, a Christian's standard is excellence and not mediocrity.

c.) Let's remember God's eyes are always watching **(Heb 4:13).**

Excellence with Family (1st Tim 5:8)

a.) Some times in our effort to be excellent in so many areas of life we unintentionally neglect our families.
b.) The bible has a strong warning for us in Timothy that it is especially important to maintain a standard of excellence with family.
c.) Even Jesus' first miracle, turning water into wine, was a boring family chore that Jesus did excellently and gave his best effort **(John 2:1-11).**

Questions:
1.) In what ways if any have you had a double standard in excellence?
2.) What areas of your life need more attention in striving to be excellent?
3.) What are some ways you see yourself growing in excellence?

Pride & Humility

Intro: Before doing this study, please read these scriptures as homework **(Mt 18:1-5, Proverbs 11:2, 12:1, 12:15, 13:10, 13:18, 14:12, 15:12, 15:25, 15:32, 16:18 28:26, I Peter 5:5-5, Colossians 3:12, Ephesians 4:2, I Sam 15:1-23)**

Read (Luke 18:9-14)

Questions:

1. Which one of these two men had the more impressive deeds?
2. Which one was forgiven?
3. What was wrong with the attitude of the Pharisee?
4. How does God feel about our pride? Why?
5. What are some ways that we can be proud?
6. What was right with the attitude of the tax collector?
7. Why is humility so important to God?
8. What are some practical ways to display our humility?
9. Would the people closest to you (Parents, teachers, friends, siblings, girlfriend, wife, children, etc.) say that you resemble the Pharisee or the tax collector the most? Why?
10. What do you need to change to be more humble?

Persecution

Intro: (II Timothy 3:12-13) If we serve Jesus we will be persecuted.

Righteousness Will Lead to Persecution (Luke 6:20-26, Acts 4:18-22, Acts 5:27-42)

Questions:

1. Why does righteousness lead to persecution?
2. According to (**Luke 6:20-26**), what should our attitude be when we are persecuted?
3. What was the attitude of the apostles? What can we learn from their approach?

Persecution Will Hit Close to Home (Mt 10:32-39, Hebrews 10:32-34, 35-39)

Questions:

1. (**Mt 10:34-36**) What did Jesus mean when he said that he didn't come to bring peace but a sword?
2. How can Jesus cause tension between Christians and their unsaved family and friends?
3. Have you experienced this? How? How does it make you feel? Has it caused you to doubt? How does Jesus expect you to approach it?
4. (**Hebrews 10:32-34**) What kind of persecution did the Christians in this passage face?
5. Have you ever faced persecution at school? At your job?
6. (**Hebrews 10:35-39**) How can persecution effect our confidence?
7. What are some keys to being the kind of disciples who do not shrink back?

Additional Scriptures

Below is a list of scriptures for further study. While this list is far from exhaustive, it should provide for much fruitful study. Enjoy.

Love	Unity	Grace/Forgiveness
I Peter 4:8	Psalm 133:1	Proverbs 17:9
John 13:34-35	John 17:20-23	Proverbs 17:14
John 15:12	Ephesians 4:2-3	Romans 14:13
Romans 13:8	Romans 12:16	Galatians 6:2
I Corinthians 12:25	Romans 15:5	I Thessalonians 5:15
II John 1:5	Galatians 5:15	I John 1:7
I Thessalonians 3:12	Galatians 5:26	Romans 12-14-21
I Thessalonians 4:18	Romans 12:5	Matthew 5:38-39
II Thessalonians 1:3	I Corinthians 1:10	Matthew 5:43-48
I Peter 1:22 I	I Corinthians 12:25	
John 3:11	Philippians 4:2	
I John 3:16	I Peter 3:8	
I John 3:23	John 17:20-21	
I John 4:7		
I John 4:11-12		
I John 4:19-21		

Forgiveness	Confession	Compassion
Ephesians 4:32	Proverbs 28:13	I Thessalonians 4:18
Colossians 3:13	James 5:16	Ephesians 4:32
Romans 15:7	I John 1:9	Colossians 3:12
I Thessalonians 5:15	Numbers 5:5-7	

Advice	Patience/Humility	The Tongue
Proverbs 11:2	Proverbs 18:13	Ephesians 4:29
Proverbs 11:14	Ephesians 4:2	Proverbs 18:21
Proverbs 12:15	Philippians 2:1-5	Proverbs 26:20
Proverbs 13:10	Galatians 5:26	Proverbs 16:28
Proverbs 14:12	Romans 14:13	James 3:1-12
Proverbs 15:22	Ephesians 5:21	Ephesians 5:19
Proverbs 19:20	Colossians 3:13	James 4:11
I Kings 12:1-33	Ecclesiastes 7:8	James 5:9
		Proverbs 15:4
		Proverbs 10:19
		Colossians 3:8

Teaching/Correction	Friendship	Discipling
Proverbs 12:1	Proverbs 17:17	Proverbs 28:26
Proverbs 13:18	Proverbs 18:24	Proverbs 13:20
Proverbs 15:12	Proverbs 27:17	Matthew 28:19-20
Colossians 3:16 I	Ephesians 4:8-12	Proverbs 19:8
I Thessalonians 5:11	Ecclesiastes 4:8-12I I	I Corinthians 4:17
Hebrews 3:13	I Samuel 20: 41-42	I Kings 19:19-21
Romans 15:14	I Samuel 23:15-18	Mark 3:13-18
Romans 14:19	II Corinthians 2:12-13	John 15:13-17
	Ruth 1:16-18	

Truth	Conflict
Proverbs 28:23	Matthew 18:15-17
Proverbs 27:5-6	Matthew 5:23-24
Proverbs 4:25	I Corinthians 6:1-11
Proverbs 4:15	Proverbs 18:17
Colossians 3:9	
Proverbs 12:19	
Ephesians 4:15	
Ephesians 4:25	

Encouragement	Serving
Romans 12:10	Galatians 5:13
Hebrews 10:24	I Peter 4:9
Hebrews 10:25	John 13:1-17
Hebrews 3:13	
I Thessalonians 5:11	

Bibliography

Coleman, Robert E. <u>The Master Plan of Evangelism</u> 2nd ed. Grand Rapids: Fleming H. Revell a division of Baker Book House Company, 1963.

Davis, F. Barton. <u>Closer Than a Brother</u> Pelham: Magi Media Publication, 2008.

Ferguson, Gordon. <u>Discipling.</u> Woburn: Discipling Publications International, 1997

Jones, Milton Lee. <u>Discipling the Multiplying Ministry.</u> Ft. Worth: Star Bible & Tract Corp., 1982

<u>The Hebrew-Greek Key Word Study Bible</u>. Chattanooga: AMG Publishers, 1996

http://www.straightdope.com/columns/read/651/has-a-human-child-ever-been-raised-by-wolves-or-other-animals (June 11, 2009)

http://www.dailymail.co.uk/news/article-503736/Werewolf-boy--snarls-bites--run-police-escaping-Moscow-clinic.html (June 11, 2009)

CPSIA information can be obtained
at www.ICGtesting.com
Printed in the USA
LVOW12s0204251117
557348LV00004BA/395/P